NOT FOR SALE

LEADING LADIES

Best wishes.

[signature]

ROHINI RATHOUR

I_AM SELF-PUBLISHING

🐦 @iamselfpub
www.iamselfpublishing.com

Contents

INTRODUCTION

TURNING A PASSION INTO A VOCATION

ENTREPRENEURSHIP: FINDING AND GROWING YOUR BUSINESS NICHE

MUMTREPRENEURS: MUMS WHO BECAME HOMEGROWN ENTREPRENEURS

GIVERS: SOCIAL ENTERPRISE AND PHILANTHROPY

LIFE LESSONS: FINDING YOUR PLACE IN THE PUZZLE

This book is a tribute to every person who has touched my life, knowingly or not, bringing me to where I am today. In particular, I dedicate this book to my husband Gurdeep, my children Ayesha, Sonaali and Yuvraj, my parents Bhalchandra and Bharati, my aunt and uncle Nirmala and Gurudutt with whom I have always had a home away from home, Nicolas Paravicini, the man who gave me my first proper career break, and last but not least Jennifer Ramsey, the best colleague and friend I could have ever wished for.

"Story is the song line of a person's life. We need to sing it and we need someone to hear the singing. Story told. Story heard. Story written. Story read creates the web of life in words."

— Christina Baldwin, *Storycatcher*

Introduction

CHAPTER 1

My Story

I spent 20 years in an industry that is all about managing money. I was a Fund Manager and my job was to invest our clients' money. At the end of 2014, I decided to call time on a job that I had thought would be for life. In the months leading up to that decision it had dawned on me that too many things had changed, it was time to be brave. Greatly influenced by Stephen Covey's *The Seven Habits of Highly Effective People*, I hoped to spend my career break developing Habit 7: Sharpen the Saw.

According to the author, "Sharpening the Saw means preserving and enhancing the greatest asset you have: you. It means having a balanced program for self-renewal in the four areas of your life: physical, social/emotional, mental, and spiritual. As you renew yourself in each of the four areas, you create growth and change in your life. Sharpening the Saw keeps you fresh so you can continue to practice the other six habits. You increase your capacity to produce and handle the challenges around you. Without this renewal, the body becomes weak, the mind mechanical, the emotions raw, the spirit insensitive, and the person selfish."

It took me several years to find the 'right' job. I used to wake up each working day looking forward to what the stock markets had in store for me. I thrived on the fact that no two days were ever the same. I had the opportunity to learn new skills, master different roles and carve out my own niche from where I could add value. The 'market' over the years provided a recurring lesson in humility. I faced three major 'bear markets' in my time, each one teaching me new lessons and providing a valuable perspective.

I met clever, hard-working people at the top of their game who represented organisations that have changed the way in which we live our lives. I learnt something new every day. In my capacity as fund manager, I was sometimes able to influence the way they ran their businesses. How many jobs are there that give you that sort of privilege, power and responsibility? One of the many rewarding aspects of my job was watching companies I had invested in achieve the potential I believed they possessed.

But I never grew up dreaming of becoming a fund manager or working in finance. In fact, where it all began could not have been further from where I am today.

The early years: living with change

I grew up in India and came from a family of servicemen. My paternal grandfather served in the Royal Indian Navy, my father and two of his three brothers also served in the Indian Navy and the Indian Army. For the sake of her children's education, my grandmother lived in Mumbai, whilst my grandfather travelled to wherever his job took him. It cannot have been easy for her spending many years in a one-bedroom flat with five children, especially as four of them were boisterous boys. There are stories of how she had to tie the furniture down to stop her children from dragging chairs or tables to the balcony that overlooked onto a busy road from three floors above.

My grandfather was an austere man of deep integrity. His own experience of spending many years away from his family was a reason why he pioneered a centralised educational standard, which aimed at helping families of peripatetic service personnel in India. This resulted in schools being set up in major cities across the country that followed the same national curriculum with standard textbooks and enabled children to join from another school, even if they were part way through their academic year. These were named *Kendriya Vidyalaya* (Central Schools).

My brother and I owe a huge debt of gratitude to my grandfather and his colleagues because they made it possible for us to travel with our father every two or three years, with very little disruption to our education, to places where his job as a Naval Officer took him.

When you live with so much change, you experience many things that leave no lasting impression. Even though I remember some things clearly, like they happened yesterday, there are great swathes of other things and details of people who touched my life that have now simply disappeared from my memory.

I remember a maths teacher at a school in Delhi who took an irrational dislike towards me. She enjoyed humiliating me by calling me to the front and getting me to work out a problem on the blackboard, knowing full well that I would fail. I don't remember her name, but I will never forget how she made me feel: fearful and ashamed.

I told my mother about this teacher, hoping she would tell her to back off. Instead, my mother suggested that I focus on improving myself by spending 10-15 minutes doing maths after school. You can just imagine how well that suggestion went down with the twelve-year-old me.

At first, I was bitterly disappointed that my mother was not willing to fight for me. Her reasoning was that if I got better at maths the teacher would leave me alone and I had no choice but to acquiesce. A few weeks later, when I did particularly well on a test, my teacher turned to me and asked me if I had cheated. More importantly, just as my mother had said, once I was no longer a soft target, she stopped picking on me.

I moved to a school in Mumbai in the next academic year, where I had one of my best ever maths teachers, whose name I do remember. Mr Balani, with his happy smiling face, instilled in me a love for the subject that lives with me even today.

That experience as a young pre-teenager taught me one of the greatest of life lessons.

Choose your battles with care. Sometimes you can win simply by making yourself stronger, so the enemy has no appetite to fight you anymore.

Coming to England: an accidental immigrant

Growing up, I had no desire to live abroad, nor did I have any aspirations of a foreign education. Many of my fellow students were busy taking entrance exams that would enable them to study in the West with a scholarship. It was the gateway to a world of opportunity, meritocracy and abundance. These educational migrants were unlikely to return home. I did not want to be one of them.

I was at a family wedding in Mumbai when I bumped into an elderly gentleman who was well known in our community for being a very good astrologer. He was trusted because he read horoscopes as a hobby, never for money. All he needed was your exact time and date of birth. Based on that information, he was able to read what the stars had in store for you. His guidance was particularly useful when parents were trying to find a suitable match for their sons or daughters. This was often the starting point in a process that could result in nuptials if the boy and girl liked each other. My parents had handed my details to him in the hope that I would let them find me a suitable husband.

Anyway, I digress. I was making small talk with the said gentleman, when he told me that he saw me working with money, and I would live abroad. I smiled politely and thanked him for this, but privately I thought he was finally losing the plot. I saw myself living in India and working in sales and marketing, once I had completed my postgraduate studies.

The Indian Institutes of Management (IIMs) were amongst the elite business schools in those days and by some miracle, I had managed to get a place in two of these. There were only four of them in the country at the time: in Ahmedabad, Bangalore, Calcutta and Lucknow. I had a choice between Calcutta and Bangalore and chose the latter for its cooler climate.

Upon graduation from IIM-B in 1991, my fellow graduates joined the 'milk rounds', an opportunity for companies to recruit some of the brightest and most promising business minds in India into their graduate trainee programmes. I chose not to participate and instead decided to join my parents in London where my father was Naval Attaché in the Indian High Commission. Armed with my new business qualifications, I had no doubt that I would land a job in London and be able to return within a year to India with some British work experience under my belt.

It was not long before I realised that no one in the UK cared a jot about my qualifications and did not see them as a reason to give me a job over and above the many thousands of British graduates who were seeking work in the depth of a full-blown recession. And who could blame them? I was wetter behind the ears than a soggy marshland.

It was a chastening experience. I began contemplating a return to India with nothing to show for my stay in England, other than the hours spent watching daytime TV, reading books from my local library and a road trip to Europe with my family. I wondered if I would make history, not in a good way, by being the only IIM graduate who failed to get a job, even back in her own home country. It was a bleak time and I started to contemplate my life as a failure, even before it had really begun.

It was during those dark days in October 1991 that I happened to come across an opportunity to work in the insurance industry as a sales representative. I was ecstatic. It did not matter that I would be working on a commission-only basis or that I would be cold-calling complete strangers. It did not even matter that I knew nothing about the financial products I was going to sell; there would be training for that. After months of waiting, I now had a reason to get up in the morning. Finally, here was an opportunity to learn, earn and put some work experience on my CV, which would be invaluable when I returned home to get a proper job!

I soon discovered that I was setting out with a clear disadvantage: an Indian accent that proved a dead giveaway over the phone. Even if the person at the other end of the phone was feeling kind towards a pesky cold caller, my accent betrayed my foreignness and my lack of understanding of British telephone etiquette. I have always been musical and good at picking up new accents. Learning to sound more British was one of the first lessons in a long list of things I learnt in the coming years.

I doggedly carried on in my job, regardless of being rather hopeless at selling. I studied the products I was meant to sell in excruciating detail, but remained unclear about their merits to the buyer. I was not too troubled by my failure, as I was not planning to make a career of this. I considered it a character building exercise with a finite end date. Then one day, I met someone who changed the entire trajectory of my life.

I had been in my job for about four months when I was introduced to a new manager who had been headhunted from another insurance firm. He seemed self-assured, had an easy manner and an infectious laugh. He was of Indian origin but spoke like a proper Brit and had anglicised his Sikh first name. This, to my overly patriotic Indian mind, was sacrilege: a sign of someone who was ashamed of his roots. I was further irritated by the fact that my boss had so freely offered him the use of my desk, presumably because I was the most junior (and therefore the most dispensable) member of staff. But he very graciously refused to uproot me from where I was seated and found himself another desk.

Over the following weeks, I got to know him better and discovered he was like no man I had ever met before. He was my manager but he also became my mentor and friend: someone who believed in me more than I believed in myself. He saw things in me that I could not see. He taught me things that have stayed with me even to this day. Despite being born and brought up in London, his heart was deeply Indian. His spoken Punjabi was old-fashioned and melodic, quite unlike what I had heard in India. He was not ashamed to speak Hindi, even if it was bitty and laced with a Punjabi accent. He was a man completely comfortable in his own skin and truly at home in a country that was foreign to me. He was also in a long-term relationship and had a daughter: a most gorgeous, bubbly little girl who clearly adored him, and he her.

So this was no Bollywood love story. My parents were horrified when I told them I had met a man who was already in a relationship and had a child. They remained vehemently opposed to the idea of us being together until they met his daughter. They melted when they saw the lovely interaction he had with his child. This was not a man who was going to abandon his daughter, even if he was no longer going to be living with her mother.

We got married in May 1993, in a simple but beautiful Sikh ceremony, attended by a handful of close family and friends. After we were married, I had a quiet moment to myself when it hit me that my life would never be the same again. It was like hitting a reset button, not knowing what would happen next.

Having never wanted to live anywhere but in India, I was now a married woman with a ready-made family in a foreign country with none of my old friends. What's more, I had almost no immediate family, once my parents returned to India, and zero career prospects. But I did have one thing that mattered more than anything else: a life partner who believed in me and loved me enough to give up the life he knew. And for that reason, I was happy to give up my country, my family and everything else that had been connected to my life before.

Career building: starting from zero

With no real career plan or relevant British qualifications, I was at a loss as to where to begin. So I registered myself at an agency for temporary jobs. Fortunately, there was no shortage of these, as long as I was prepared to do the most menial of administrative tasks, such as filing, data input, answering the telephone working in a call centre or being a receptionist.

The next four years were deeply formative ones for me. As a temporary worker, you are in a rather special place: you can be friendly without really seeking to make friends and be professional without appearing to be too keen to progress within the firm. As long as you show up and do your job, no one really pays attention to you. I became computer literate on the job, despite having never used a computer before. I also learnt to recognise and appreciate British humour, and I assimilated into the local working culture in my own way. It was the perfect grounding for me to observe and I was able to absorb things that no amount of money or special schooling could ever have taught me.

You may wonder why I persisted with temping for so long. I wanted to find a job that was 'the one' for me; one that I would love and want to stay in for years to come. In the absence of such a job opportunity, I thought it was best to keep on temping in the hope that each successive assignment would take me closer to the right permanent job.

There were times when I despaired. I could not believe that after all my years of education back in India, I had amounted to so little. At these times I was buoyed by my husband's continued faith that I would find my true calling some day, and he willed me not to give up.

Alongside working, I had started studying for Investment Management qualifications, which I prepared for in my own time at home. Thanks to a dear friend of my husband's, I spent many months getting work experience as a research analyst at his fund management firm that specialised in Emerging Markets.

With some relevant qualifications and work experience under my belt, I started applying to jobs in the City of London, the financial heartbeat of the UK. There were failed interviews, but every rejection taught me a new lesson in what not to do in front of a prospective employer. It was only later in life that I realised those setbacks saved me for the one opportunity that was right for me.

In April 1997, I met with a headhunter who changed my life. R Kelly's song *I Believe I Can Fly* was on the radio, the morning I set out for my job interview with a small portfolio management firm. I started my first proper job as Assistant Fund Manager on 19th May 1997, just over six years after I first came to England. True to my quest to find a job for life, I stayed with the same firm for 18 years.

Motherhood

I remember being asked in my job interview if I might be starting a family in the next year or two. My interviewer explained that although this would be a happy development for me, it would be a disaster for a small company like theirs to lose me so soon after my appointment. Such a question would spark outrage in the current politically correct environment and be thoroughly condemned as being sexist. But in all honesty, I was glad my interviewer had asked me so that I could answer him with candour. It was much better to have it out in the open than him to harbour doubts about this and deny me the job because of it. I told him how long I had waited to find the right career path and so having a baby was furthest from my mind now that I had this opportunity. Thankfully, he believed me and the job was mine to keep.

When we were expecting our first child in 2000, my husband and I discussed at length the best way forward. We were both in demanding jobs with little chance of either working part-time or from home. We didn't have family nearby who we could rely on, and leaving our baby with a complete stranger while we were out at work seemed unfair. In addition, professional childcare was, and still is, hugely expensive. The idea of giving up the job that I was thriving in made me sad, but I would have done it had there been no other option.

My husband did a wonderful thing for me. He offered to quit his job and stay at home full-time to look after our baby. His reasoning was that he had been working for over 20 years and he was happy to take a break. I, on the other hand, had only just begun my career and he believed I had a lot further to rise. He had also been a hands-on father with his first child and knew more about babies and their needs than I did as a first-time mum.

Knowing our daughter was in her father's good hands every single day made it easier for me to leave home before anyone else was awake and return in the evening, after spending a full and productive day at work. He continued to be the full-time parent to both our children for 15 years. It is only recently he has found himself a job that is giving him a chance to build a new chapter in his working life.

Work-life balance

Being in a full-time job, with increasing levels of responsibility, was sometimes stressful and I never could completely switch off. But I did my best not to bring my work home, so the precious hours I spent with my family were theirs alone.

Once I was home, the kids were my responsibility. Homework, bath time, reading to them at bedtime and staying with them until they fell asleep were my ways of keeping the bond alive. I loved those hours when my daughter would talk to me about her day at school: the friendships she had made and lost, and made again; her little battles on the playground or the kindness another child had bestowed upon her. My son was less chatty and the reasons for that became clear to us when he was about four years old. He was diagnosed as being on the autistic spectrum. His speech was very delayed and to this day he is far less likely to volunteer information about his day at school.

Fund management has always been a male-dominated industry but unlike some women in the City, I was the sole breadwinner for my family and that made me think like a man. I enjoyed my work and was good at it. But it was not always easy. I promised myself that I would stay in the job for as long as I had new things to learn and woke up each day looking forward to what lay in store for me.

In 2014, there was a perfect storm of events in my personal life and at work. My children were growing up. The connection I had with them when they were much younger needed to be replaced with something more relevant to their needs now they were older. Being at home for so long was having a detrimental impact on my husband; he needed to get out there and find a new reason to get up every morning. In addition, I started to feel stifled in my workplace, so the decision to quit never felt more right.

Life after work

The early days of being a full-time stay at home mum were bliss. No more alarm clocks going off at some ungodly hour. No more fumbling through the wardrobe in the dark, so as to not disturb the rest of the family, who were still asleep.

No more daily commute on a train service that broke down when there were 'leaves on the tracks' or we had the 'wrong kind of snow'.

I loved being able to wake my kids up, make them breakfast and walk my younger one to school in what was his final year of primary school. We would talk about the colours in the sky, the sound of chirping birds and other little things that matter when you are a child. Some days we would walk in silence, occasionally speaking to greet a friend who was also heading towards the school. It is one of the many things I am so grateful for: having the chance to spend those months walking my son to and from school, and learning things about his life that I never previously had the time for.

Once back home, I would zone in on household chores with gusto, as I found washing dishes and cleaning therapeutic. The hours stretched in front of me, like a fresh piece of parchment waiting for me to fill in as I chose. I soon found myself projects to work on, things I knew I would not have the chance to do once I was back at work. I started to cook more and trained to become a hoop-dance fitness teacher. I had more time for friends and family. Most of all, it was an opportunity to simply take a break from the life I had known for so long.

I gained a new-found respect for anyone who is a stay at home parent. The hardest thing about being at home all day is that, although you seem to have a whole day to yourself, there are endless chores that need doing that you don't get paid for. Just because you no longer have a job does not mean you are not working. I discovered that it made sense not to have everything in perfect order all the time so the family would notice when the house was clean and tidy. As the months have worn on, jobs around the house have lost their therapeutic quality, as they have slid back into just being chores.

Working life for me used to be an unending series of deadlines. Some were pre-set but a number simply cropped up and demanded to be met. Despite days when nothing went to plan, I am proud to say that I never missed an important deadline at work. Now that I am at home, I have the freedom to choose what I do, when I do it, and if I do it at all on any given day. I occasionally miss the buzz of the externally created drama and the sense of not knowing what might happen next. Most of all, I miss the deadlines.

With that realisation, I knew I was ready to find my next challenge feeling refreshed, renewed and with my 'saw sharpened'. A new challenge, one where I could create my own deadlines (at least to begin with) and become my own boss. Writing this book is the first really important step towards that goal.

CHAPTER 2

This book

Like a number of my decisions in life, writing a book was not something I had ever planned or thought I was even capable of doing. I lack the imagination to be a fiction writer, but I discovered during my working years that I enjoy writing and can bring concepts and stories to life with my words.

If someone had asked me as an 18-year-old to write down what I thought I would be doing 30 years later, I doubt I would have got even a single thing right. That is what makes life so interesting. Few of us can ever really predict our own future, let alone someone else's.

Our lives are full of *Sliding Door* moments, like in the movie where we are shown two alternate developments in the character's life, depending on whether she caught the tube home one day or missed it. Years of planning and preparation can sometimes seem a waste if they do not result in the outcome we had hoped for. My experience tells me that almost nothing we do is ever a waste if it teaches us something new or makes us stronger.

This book explores the stories of 32 women and one man (who tells us his late mother's story and the impact she had on his own life) in different stages of their lives, providing the reader with a broad spectrum of backgrounds, aspirations and achievements. I wanted to hear their back story: what their early experiences were, what it was like growing up, what motivated them, who they turned to for support and encouragement, their life's vision, the lessons they learnt and the advice they had for others.

A number of those I approached were known to me. Others were recommended by friends or had approached me because they felt my project chimed with them. Many of the women I interviewed for this book were speaking to me for the very first time. I wanted them to feel at ease and open up in a way that felt right to them. I am grateful for the trust they placed in me and I hope I have done justice to their stories.

Some of the ladies in this book have already 'arrived' at the place they want to be, others are still finding their way, and still others are on their second or third journey. For this reason, not every story will flow the same. I hope the personalities of these individual women will shine through their words and my narration of their stories. Some were open and chatty, while others left more to the imagination, but proved no less insightful for their reticence.

At first, it was not my intention to include my story at all, but then I realised that without it, the reader might find it harder to understand my motivation for writing this book and the conclusions at the end. I am guilty of verbal diarrhoea when it comes to the narration of my own story, which aims to provide the reader with a glimpse into my life's journey and how I got to the place where I find myself today.

It took exactly three months, from the very first interview to the first draft of the book being finished. I decided not to plan the structure of the book nor place the ladies into any predetermined buckets before I had spoken to every one of them, got their approval on how I intended to tell their story, and read every one of the stories in alphabetical order.

Their stories of resilience, compassion and courage tell us that there is nothing in this world that stops us from discovering the person we are meant to be, or from becoming the person we want to be, even if it takes us an entire lifetime to get there. This is the kind of self-help book that enables you to look at your own life through the prism of someone else's experience.

You may relate to the places that the protagonists in this book found themselves in during various points in their lives, and you could draw parallels to your own situation.

You could learn from their mistakes, understanding full well that it won't stop you from making your own. You will learn that making mistakes and failure are all part of a learning process that never ends.

You may be in an unhappy place, too afraid of the unknown to make a change or walk away from things that are making you sad. You are not alone. Others have been there too and have found the "unknown" is not such a bad place, once you get there. But it needs courage and a certain mindset to take that first step. You could draw inspiration from their journey.

I also hope this book will shine a light on the subject of women's contribution to society and economic growth. It is often less visible, can be intangible and is therefore frequently underappreciated. Women will always play the role of nurturers and playmakers from the shadows, enjoying none of the glory. Just because they don't get paid or receive any formal recognition for their role should not stop us from acknowledging their worth.

Most of all, this book aims to help us see why this world needs both men and women. We each have a role to play. Women's empowerment is not about having to prove that we are equal to men, or better than them. It has everything to do with understanding, accepting and celebrating who we are, what makes us different, how we complement each other, and ultimately how best we can each contribute to this world in our own unique way.

CHAPTER 3

The puzzle of life

Imagine a gigantic jigsaw puzzle. There are pieces scattered all over and no pre-drawn picture to help you complete it. New pieces are getting added all the time, even as prevailing ones move, change or disappear. Now imagine that each one of us on this planet is a unique piece of this complex and evolving jigsaw puzzle.

From the moment we are born, our quest in life is to discover where we fit so as to complete a tiny portion of the picture that relates to our own life. Our choices and actions, how we react to events outside our control will determine what sort of person we become. Over our lifetime, we will build a unique tapestry of pictures that make up the different stages: childhood, growing up, getting a job, finding a life partner, parenthood and so on. Every one of these will represent milestones in a lifelong journey to find our place in this world.

Finding mentors who help us to see things that we may be blind to is a blessing. You are never too young or too old to benefit from this. A part of our life's journey is to seek out teachers and mentors: be they in our workplace, amongst friends or closer to home within our family.

In due course, it may be our turn to become mentors and coaches to others. Helping someone to either learn a skill that will change their life or become the person they have the potential to be is one of the most rewarding and effective ways of giving.

My first teachers were my parents who instilled in me values that have stayed with me. After I came to England, it was my husband who became my mentor in a foreign land. He also became the wind beneath my wings, helping me rise to heights that I could never have achieved alone.

Now it is my turn to start again. This time as a teacher, mentor and coach to those who might benefit from my knowledge and experience.

It is never too late to take control of the puzzle that is your life. No one else can solve it for you; you alone must make the journey in search of your place and find the other pieces that complete your picture.

Turning a passion into a vocation

How many of us have always known what we wanted to be when we grew up, and how many of those have gone on to achieve their childhood dream?

What happens if you get there and discover it is nothing like you had expected it would be? Imagine having to start all over again. Even if our early choices of where we want to be don't come to pass, they can help us to discover what we are good at, what we love doing and whether it is valued enough for us to make a living from it.

Whether you are a student at a critical juncture in your academic journey, someone who feels trapped in a career or a housewife who has never worked but now wants to gain financial independence, it is never too late to rediscover what we are good at, make time for things that we are passionate about and find ways to seek fulfilment from them.

Not everything we do in life needs to have a financial outcome attached to it. Not everyone will be fortunate to make a decent living out of things they have a passion for. It may be that you are fortunate enough not to be the main breadwinner in your household. Spending time doing things that you love can have many benefits, most of which have nothing to do with money.

What follows is the stories of women whose career choices were moulded by their childhood experiences and steered by what they once believed was their destiny. In some cases, they made the right academic choices that prepared them for a job they loved doing and had a natural propensity for. Others just had a raw talent that was nurtured within a supportive network of family and friends, and then turned into a passion that now fuels their working life.

CHAPTER 4

Ann Wright – Managing Director, Rough House Media – The UK

Ann has over two decades of media experience that she now uses to help clients with their communication strategies, including public relations, crisis communication and social media.

Ann knew she wanted to become a journalist when she worked on a student newspaper publication and wrote her first ever article. She spent the first ten or so years as a newspaper journalist before moving to the BBC, where she worked in news, investigative documentaries and covering high-profile events, such as royal weddings. It was a hugely satisfying and enjoyable job, but at the same time could be demanding and stressful, involving long and unpredictable hours.

Motherhood and changed priorities

After the birth of her son in 2008, Ann decided she didn't want to juggle TV production and motherhood, and found she could not do full justice to either. Ann and her husband had already been running a small business called Rough House Media alongside their day jobs, offering training courses in media interviews and crisis communications. She took this over with the aim of growing it to replace her full-time income. At the time she took on the mantle of running Rough House, it had a core of clients that offered her good repeat business, which gave Ann a good starting point.

Despite having been in high-pressure situations producing high-quality TV programming, running her own business took Ann out of her own comfort zone. She enjoyed the challenge and relished the flexibility of being able to work from home, where she could care for her young son.

"At first, I was terrified of cold calling," says Ann. "Then one day I looked at the biography of the person I was ringing and saw that she had only 2-3 years experience. I told myself I had no reason to be nervous given all the knowledge I had gained in my years in the media." She also remembers the time she got news of her first ever client win. "I danced around the room with joy," says Ann laughing.

In the early days, she got advice from Business Link, a government-run organisation targeting small business owners in the UK. She also created her own network of contacts via social media for business advice. Three years ago Ann started to work with a business coach who helped her to think and run her business more strategically.

Customer-driven expansion

At first, Ann focused on the traditional media training services that were Rough Media's main offering. By listening to customer feedback and responding to their needs, her business offering has expanded. She now offers a number of related and adjacent services, including additional training courses, creating crisis communication strategies, producing content, such as videos, podcasts and articles, social media, and providing PR support. She also offers training courses in partnership with industry bodies, such as the PRCA, on how to write your own press releases, how to do your own PR, crisis communications and manage your social media presence.

Ann doesn't advertise anymore, as she finds word of mouth, referrals and social media more effective. She prides herself on maintaining a personalised relationship with her clients whom she has always had good feedback from.

Competition vs. collaboration

Ann concurs that there are "hundreds of companies that do what we do". But Ann has carved out a niche focusing primarily on clients who are not-for-profit, and now she has a particular expertise in that area. She deliberately chose this sphere because "we like working for people who have something worthwhile to say and it fits with our own values and principles." Her eight original clients included some in the education sector and industry membership bodies, and she has gone on to expand her clientele along the same lines.

Ann is a believer in collaboration, especially with organisations that are complementary to her own. For instance, Ann partners with PR firms and works with organisations that use her business to train their members. Working with leading industry bodies gives her credibility, generates awareness of her business and is more likely to put her in contact with people she wants to work with than blanket advertising ever could.

How does Ann create these new service offerings and what gives her the confidence to proceed? She gives an example. We live in an age of real-time information when bad news can spread fast and sink reputations if it is not handled correctly. "We moved into doing crisis communications and started to look at how we could do things differently," she says. "Our knowledge, as journalists, of covering crises means we have a really good insight into how the media behaves during an emergency. We tried out our approach with one client and found it went really well." That success gave Ann the confidence to roll out this new service with her own crisis communications strategy.

Building a team of freelance professionals

Rough House employs skilled media professionals on a freelance basis. Her website features an A-list team of people who have worked across all the different aspects of media, social media and communications. This breadth of talent enables her to match her client's needs with the right personality and skillset.

Has she found the work-life balance she was seeking at the outset? "Last year was very busy. But luckily for me, my husband works in 24-hour news so his shift patterns give us the flexibility to juggle our home life with work," says Ann. Working from home can have its moments. She remembers an occasion one Friday afternoon when her son had a friend over to their house for a play date, accompanied by his little brother and mum. Ann and the mum were chatting over a glass of wine when the phone rang. "It was a PR firm with a client who had a crisis that needed dealing with. A former employee had sent a malicious email to all journalists and the client needed advice on how to respond," remembers Ann. Mental and emotional agility are the order of the day when you are a mum and working from home.

Under Ann's leadership, the business has grown from eight clients to almost 70, including multinationals and globally respected organisations. As a company, hers is punching above its weight, even though she runs it from a room in her home. She does most things herself but admits there are some things she finds harder than others, such as sales and search engine optimisation (SEO).

Lessons learnt and advice

- "Network strategically."
- "Think carefully where you want your clients to come from so you can specialise in a niche."
- "Find a supportive peer group and use it to share experiences." Ann found hers via social media.

"When setting up a business you need to know what you are talking about. Go with what you know and what you are good at."

CHAPTER 5

Claire Boscq-Scott – Founder, The Busy Queen Bee – Jersey

Claire has turned her lifelong passion for working in the hospitality industry into a business that focuses on helping her corporate clients to put customer service at the heart of their business.

Claire grew up in France and from the age of seven loved helping out in her father's restaurant. Hospitality was clearly in her DNA as she chose to work in that industry doing a number of "seasonal" jobs that gave her the opportunity to travel.

She arrived in Jersey for the first time 24 years ago. From Jersey, she travelled to America where she worked in a Disney resort and got her first real experience of customer service in a culture that aims at "creating an amazing experience for the customer every step of the way".

Claire returned to Jersey a few years later – married and with her first child – and went back to work in the hotel industry. During this time she experienced the phenomenon of "mystery shoppers" who were hired by her employer to independently assess the quality of the customer service within the organisation.

She had observed that this was a service not locally available on the island at the time. Her employer was paying rather a lot for mystery shoppers to travel from the UK to Jersey. Not only was this expensive, but it was also less than perfect because they were from the mainland and so did not truly represent the local population.

Marital breakdown and her light bulb moment

Claire has two children and was going through a divorce. "Hospitality in the hotel industry is non-stop. There was no work-life balance." Now a single parent, she simply could not carry on as before.

The idea for her current business came to her when she was taking an early morning walk whilst on a break with some of her girlfriends. She calls it her "light bulb moment" when she suddenly saw clearly how she could put her skills and experience to work. Within two months she had put together a business plan and a month later handed in her notice to her then employer.

At first, Claire had four separate business ideas all of which drew upon her own previous work experience: wedding planning, event planning, marketing services and mystery shopping services. Her children were only six and ten at the time, so she wanted to start a business that gave her the flexibility to work from home around their school days and holidays.

Due to the difficult personal circumstances in which the business idea was conceived, she did not have time to test the market first. Claire says she "just took the leap because it felt so right." She knew there was a demand for mystery shopping services that was not being met locally. The other three service areas were Claire's way of spreading the risk, in the hope that at least one of them would work out.

Early experiences

How did she get the business off the ground in the early days and weeks? Claire had some initial help and support from the Enterprise Body, a Jersey government organisation aimed at helping small businesses. She also networked relentlessly and "mystery shopped" other businesses, as she tried to understand how they operated and what they charged for their services.

Within a couple of years, she realised that the mystery shopper business was the one with the greatest potential for growth. Her first client in Jersey also had shops in Guernsey and the Isle of Man, thereby broadening her potential market to beyond the island of Jersey. She discovered that the other islands had a similar lack of local supply when it came to mystery shopping services, especially as most local businesses had never really given customer service quite as much thought.

In the early years, her greatest challenge was to make her target market of local businesses understand both the importance of customer service and the role that mystery shopping plays in improving it. Many business owners were set in their old ways and saw no reason to change, so it was not always easy persuading them that better customer service would bring long-term value to their business.

"Being a woman means you are always having to prove yourself. You end up giving so much time and advice for free." Claire recalls one time a couple of years ago when she had back-to-back meetings over a period of seven hours. Six of those were spent with people who were there simply "to pick my brains", and she even ended up paying for the coffee for one of them.

Business breakthrough: expose problems and provide solutions

Initially, Claire focused her efforts on providing mystery shoppers and then delivering the results to her customers. Soon she realised, however, that customers did not always know what to do with the findings, which often showed their failings. So Claire discovered she had a real opportunity to provide them with solutions to the problems her mystery shoppers had identified.

This proved a real turning point for Claire. Three years into starting up on her own, she had a choice now to either remain small or grow by taking on permanent staff. She also had a vision of expanding to other islands and "help others to do better" by focusing on the way they looked after their customers.

She now has a core group of customers who retain her services on an ongoing basis because they realise that customer service standards need to be sustained, not just fixed on a one-off basis. This gives her business greater certainty and means she now has the luxury of contemplating investing in the future.

It took four years for the business to generate enough revenue to pay herself a decent salary. Now she has 80 people who work for her as mystery shoppers. They include a range of men and women representing a relevant mix of the local population who work for her on a contract basis. Word of mouth has always been a powerful driver of her new business and she has never had to advertise.

She continues to work from home and has felt no need to move into a separate office. In fact, she enjoys the flexibility that having a room in her home as her office gives her. It enables her to work well into the night, if need be, and be there for her children. It also saves on costs.

Growing the business via the franchising route

At one networking event, Claire got talking about how bees operate, the importance of hives and the position of the Queen Bee. This gave her the idea of rebranding her business as the BusyQueenBee. This would enable her to potentially create a franchise, so that her services could cover the other islands that have remained insular. Serendipitously, a lawyer with expertise in creating franchises overheard this conversation and suggested he could help Claire turn this into a reality.

The decision to franchise is a huge step for any business. "When you create your business, it is your baby. Everything we do (at the BusyQueenBee) is about customer service. People buy people." She intends to "hand pick every person who will be working with her". She has put together clear and rigorous operational guidelines that should give any franchisee the tools to ensure they work to her high standards.

Does working alone ever get lonely? "Being my own boss is liberating. I have a big group of friends, and the networking has helped to build my own little tribe who are there for me."

Claire is a firm believer that "everything we do in life is about rapport, whether it is with a customer, or in our personal relationships or those we work with". Her long-term vision is to have "Bee Hives" on several islands and become a "Buzzational Speaker" who inspires others, particularly women. There would also be "Speed Buzzing" networking events, helping to connect different small businesses, so they can create "tribes" whose members become the extended support system every business owner needs.

Lessons learnt and advice

- "You need to have a real passion for what you do, but also be realistic about how you can make money from it."
- "You may need to give your time for free to begin with, but you soon need to find smarter ways to monetise your expertise."

"I wish that I had not wasted time on the three other businesses in the early years, and focused on the mystery shopping business instead. But then I could not have known which one was right for me unless I had tried them all first. I learnt so much from my mistakes."

CHAPTER 6

Deanne Love
– Co-Founder,
Hooplovers – Australia

Deanne founded Hooplovers with her husband Masao Tamaoki. They use the power of the Internet to reach a global audience of hula-hooping enthusiasts through Deanne's carefully crafted YouTube tutorials and training courses.

As a child, Deanne dreamed of becoming a primary school teacher but was also very interested in the psychology of marketing. She has three Degrees, one in Commerce, a Business Degree in Marketing and Human Resources, and a third in Education.

She started her teaching career in Australia but moved to Tokyo in 2003 in order to fulfil a childhood fantasy of living in the "coolest, busiest city in the world" and continued working there as a primary school teacher. Although she still loved teaching, she starting to feel stifled a few years later. "I was in a wild city but felt I was shrinking," says Deanne. She knew she needed a change but had no idea what else she could do.

Hoopy beginnings

Deanne picked up a hula-hoop for the very first time in 2007. She was inspired by a YouTube clip of a woman hula-hooping in her apartment. "It was a very memorable experience," she recalls, "and I thought, I could do that!"

Deanne was on the lookout for hooping classes but found none that suited her in Tokyo. She persisted with a light plastic child's hoop, not knowing at that point there was a "whole subculture around hooping" or that she could get hoops in adult sizes. "One day my mum came to visit. I was 30-years-old and she realised that I was obsessed," she remembers with a laugh.

By then Deanne had done a bit more research on the Internet and had come across a website called Hooping.org that provided information on the different kinds of adult hoops.

She bought herself some hooping DVDs and practised in her apartment or in a nearby park. "They were really basic moves, but they were challenging."

"Hooping brought out so many elements in me: creativity, dance and movement. It shone a light on aspects that I knew had always been inside me." Having discovered hooping, Deanne really wanted to bring it into the community and let others have what she had found.

In 2009, Deanne took the leap and decided to quit teaching and make hooping her full-time "job". She didn't have any mentors or business coaches at that point, who could help her with the transition from being an employee to starting up her own business. What she had in abundance though was passion, even obsession, for hooping and boundless confidence. "I was totally fuelled by the desire and felt so empowered by this need to teach others. I had been a teacher for ten years and so I felt I had all the pieces to put together."

Was it a challenge to turn something that gave her such joy into a profitable business? "It needs a real understanding of the psychology of what we do. The question is how to turn a spiritual experience into a money-making venture. We can't deny that we live in a world that needs money. I navigate around the dilemma by knowing that I am not a millionaire." She points out that a huge amount of planning and hard work goes into what might look like "fun in the park" to other people. "It is always an evolution and I am always learning every day."

Although hula-hooping is at the heart of Deanne's business, her work is multi-faceted, encompassing "education, running a small business, marketing and hooping." These create pockets of creativity and growth, but Deanne can choose to switch off one or more of those things, based on what she feels that her students and customers want.

Partnership: in life and in business

Deanne's equal partner in the business is Masao Tamaoki, who is also her husband. When they first met both were in full-time jobs in Tokyo. Masao worked for a technology company but was not in IT. Not long after they'd met, he quit his job and created a business that involved helping others to go down the e-commerce route. Like Deanne's love of hooping, Masao too had a real passion for technology around e-commerce and was very much self-taught. "He loves learning all the time," says Deanne.

Deanne and Masao created Hooplovers together. Even though Deanne is the public face of the business, Masao is the force behind the scenes who created its successful platform. They built the website, the logo and much more together. Deanne is a self-confessed "daydreamer" and a "very visual" person. She would explain her vision to Masao, who would then map things out and turn them into reality. Theirs is a lovely partnership of two people who complement each other beautifully. They are also perfectionists and the attention to detail is evident in everything they put out to the public, be it videos or the online teaching courses for would-be Hoop Love coaches.

What's it like to live with someone you also work so closely with? "We are both really calm, both workaholics," she replies.

"We know how to balance and support each other and make time for a break. I have learnt to give myself a break. If you continuously push through you can get burnt out. You need to make sure that you don't get to a stage where you don't love it anymore."

Coping with calamity

The story of Hooplovers has two important chapters. The first one began in Tokyo. Deanne had managed to build a decent business from a standing start by running classes and selling hoops in the local community. She had earned the informal accolade of "the best marketer in Tokyo". Quirky but effective marketing tricks included leaving gorgeous hula-hoops in public places with a post-it note that gave details of her classes.

Her previous experience of teaching young children at primary school, and later having taught herself to hoop, made her an excellent hoop teacher who could break down complicated moves and make them accessible for her students. Her naturally bubbly personality brought fun and flow to her classes, bringing an art form that was previously often associated with circus gymnasts, into the more popular arena of dance.

Things were ticking along nicely for Deanne and Masao when the 2011 earthquake and tsunami struck Japan. It had a devastating impact on the Japanese economy. Suddenly, anything fun or non-essential was the last thing on anyone's mind in Tokyo. With heavy hearts and very little money, Deanne and Masao packed their bags and arrived in Australia.

"All we had with us was the determination to survive and our sheer passion. When your life is completely changed by a natural disaster, it is amazing to see how it is possible to just push yourself," says Deanne. "It took us a long time to come out of the trauma, but underneath that we had each other and I still loved hooping. It made us so much stronger. We got to recreate Hooplovers from the ground up."

Starting again and rebuilding

In Tokyo, the business was very local – doing workshops and dance schools. Coming to Australia was in many ways the making of Hooplovers, turning it into the global online success story that it is today. Masao's former experience of helping businesses to become e-commerce ready played a big role. He knew what it took to sell things online.

YouTube had always intrigued Deanne and Masao. Instinctively, they knew it had a role to play in promoting their business. After all, it was a hooping clip on YouTube that had inspired Deanne all those years ago. She remembers their early attempts at creating a YouTube video and the time and effort spent on making it look right, so that it would capture the mood and also become a tutorial. "We had to be really disciplined. We made a bold commitment to start creating YouTube videos once a week," says Deanne. They were responding to feedback that said Deanne needed to be the "face of Hooplovers".

"It was an idea that I was really terrified of at first," recalls Deanne. A number of little pieces were already coming together in the Hooplovers jigsaw puzzle, and building a personal brand was a very important one. They were discovering the power of social media and the personal branding became a real tool in fuelling their growth.

By now, Deanne had built up years of experience and was still passionate about Hooplovers, but she needed to put it all into a business framework. She signed up for a course that cost her $2,000. Although this was an amount they could ill afford, she viewed this as an investment in their future. The course entitled her to a business coach who proved instrumental in helping her to "be more discerning about what you want to do and how you share hooping" with others.

Is there a downside to being such a public figure? "When you put yourself out there you are in a very vulnerable place. Not everyone agrees with you." As a result, Deanne has learnt over the years to form a thicker skin. "Even though I really do care about what people think, do I care about people who are not being constructive? Sometimes it is just personal preference. Some people don't like the fact that hula-hoopers make money." Experience has taught her to just let negative things go and focus on all the positive things that life brings.

Deanne is part of a group called Mastermind Women. It comprises women from different businesses who come together to share their stories and draw inspiration from one another. She is the only hula-hooper in the group.

Deanne's vision for Hooplovers

"We are riding the wave of technology at the moment," she says. "Technology is supporting and boosting the way that we can teach. Technology allows us to give a more authentic experience." Deanne and Masao are now exploring the possibility of live streaming – powerful technologies that will allow virtual classrooms. She sees herself using Facebook Live in future to answer questions in an interactive way, rather than the pre-recorded format they currently use. "There are lots of retreats and hoop conferences around the world I would love to go to. It is challenging to get there." Live streaming could change that by expanding her reach even further and allowing her to collaborate more widely with other hoopers around the world.

Lessons learnt and Advice

- "Spend less time thinking and more time acting on ideas. Too much thinking can hold you back."
- "Reaching out, asking questions and asking for help are all powerful ways to move forward. Being a small business can leave you feeling isolated, it is important to stay connected."
- "It is really important to get out of your own community. Don't allow yourself to get blinkered."

"Be honest with yourself. Be authentic and find out who you are. Take inspiration and find your own "special sauce". Many of us don't even realise what that is. Enhance who you are."

CHAPTER 7

Harriet Waley-Cohen– Health & Wellness Coach – The UK

Harriet is a certified health coach, psychology graduate and mentor. She is an experienced public speaker, seeking to inspire and empower change through her talks and workshops.

Harriet started her career in the City of London as an investment writer at an asset management firm. She enjoyed her job and headed up a team that worked to tight deadlines and fast turnaround times. After she had children, Harriet started working for the same team on an ad hoc basis in order to keep stress levels low. She also worked as a freelance editor for a different investment firm in the City.

Harriet has two young children and a few years ago found the courage to end her marriage. It was not an easy decision but she had reached a point where she was deeply unhappy and it was the only way to regain control of her life. She needed to start again and find something that would not only allow her to support herself and her children financially, but would also work around their schedules.

Retraining

A Facebook post from a friend about to embark on a Health Coaching training programme got Harriet thinking. Harriet had been mentoring young women with addiction for about 12 years. She did it for free without any formal training, and her own successful battle with addiction in the past had made her empathetic towards others suffering the same plight.

Harriet, who has a degree in Psychology, had always been "naturally very interested in human behaviour" and the idea of becoming a health coach "chimed and felt like a good fit" because "it sat well with my wanting to make a difference and work around my children's routine."

The course was about the bigger picture on health, so it looked beyond just physical health and diet, and covered coaching skills and business skills as well. Best of all, it was all home study with ten hours of lectures from real leaders of health and wellbeing. As everyone on the course was connected through Facebook, it meant there was a community from day one, so no student felt isolated.

She then went on to do Speaker Training to help her become a more confident public speaker, where she met "a phenomenal community" of other entrepreneurs and speakers, all equally determined to make a positive difference, both in the world and in other people's lives.

Finding the ideal customer and how to price your services

The courses provided a path towards creating a sustainable source of income working from home. At first, she didn't narrow down her addressable market and instead targeted anyone who had a health problem. But soon Harriet found she had an affinity for a certain kind of person and was attracted to working with them.

With the help of some additional business coaching, she was able to further define her ideal client, even down to creating an avatar of her and working out where she liked to shop etc. Harriet, who is a huge believer in finding mentors, found herself a "fantastic business mentor" who helped to shape her business better. She also has a close-knit group of fellow professionals that share information.

Once she had clearly defined her target market, she needed to decide on what she was going to charge them. Luckily, she could turn to her network of fellow students from the Institution of Integrative Nutrition, where she did her Health Coaching training. After discussing it with her peers, she came up with a price that seemed right for someone who was just starting out. As more people started working with her and she gained credibility, Harriet was able to steadily increase her prices, so now they are three times higher than when she first started. The price increase also reflects the value of her time, as she gets more demand than she can fulfil.

What is her view on giving away stuff for free when you first start out and have no customers? "My first consultation with a potential client is always free. I also give away, for instance, small bits of coaching in the form of a newsletter and a weekly video on social media for free." But Harriet firmly believes that people do not value things they receive for nothing. The same goes for people's perception of something that is priced too low.

Not afraid to seek help

What was her experience in the early days, when she had to take care of all aspects of the business whilst also providing her clients with a service? "The business side of the course really helped. They encouraged students to set goals, make clear plans to achieve them, and to work on marketing and operations." She goes on to say, "I also don't have a problem admitting that I have no clue about something and looking for people who do know."

Some of her friends have become successful coaches and they all had their own business coaches or mentors. So she was aware that she needed one too. The mentor she found herself was very strong on "mindset" (consistency of self-belief) and very helpful on how she should present herself on stage and how to put content together. She also worked with an American coach who creates programmes for building an online business. Last but not least, she needed strategic input and so found herself a mentor who helped her with her business strategy.

Harriet is a big believer in the benefits of learning and the transformational power of having a good coach. She views them as an investment worth making. "Continuing to learn is very important. To stand still is to go backwards. I would always be happy to pay for coaching, just as my clients pay for my time."

Competition vs. collaboration

How does she view her competition? "I welcome competition! It makes you raise the game. What makes you great today makes you average tomorrow." Which is why she sets so much store on continuously improving herself and staying in close contact with her community of friends and fellow professionals. She goes on to say, "I believe in the abundance model, that there is enough business out there for us all. People are attracted to (work with) me because of who I am and because they are right for me."

How does Harriet ensure that she has a work-life balance, and how does she cope with emotionally draining days with clients? Harriet does almost all of her coaching sessions from home via Skype and works around her children's needs. The only time she travels is when she has speaking engagements. "There are some times that are sacred and no work is done. Taking that into account is how I decide on how to price my coaching programmes." She has a coach to debrief with after an emotionally charged session with a client.

Making a difference

Harriet tells me about a girl who came to her with enormous anxiety issues. She was in a destructive relationship with her body and had a fear of flying. Working closely with her revealed much deeper causes for her behaviour but the girl has turned things around completely with Harriet's help. She has changed the way she feels about her body and recently got on a long haul flight to a previously unimaginably faraway destination. Turnaround stories like hers are the reason why Harriet wanted to become a life coach.

But she cannot help every client. There are some people who come to her with problems that simply cannot be treated by coaching sessions alone. For instance, when there are addiction issues, Harriet will often refer people to others who are better qualified to help. The individual must also be willing to work with her and want to make a change.

Vision for her business

"My vision is for a global presence with a number of online courses that will undo a lot of the damage done by the media about what women's bodies should look like. Only five per cent of the women have bodies like those portrayed in the media." She is also brimming with ideas on how she can work in collaboration with others to help young girls understand the value of healthy relationships.

Lessons learnt and advice

- "Plug into a community."
- "Look to collaborate."
- "Seek advice: get a good coach or mentor."
- "Find the things you are passionate about with a problem you are looking to solve."
- "But passion is not enough, you need to be realistic."
- "Get your head around the concept of money: it is not a dirty word!"

"The lesson is not to burn out. It is a lot of time, effort and energy in the beginning, but it is really important to find me-time and take really good care of yourself. Find the things that make you well and happy."

CHAPTER 8

Kaye Dunbar – Franchisee, Travel Counsellors – The UK

Through Travel Counsellors, Kaye found an elegant way to combine becoming a business owner and doing the job she loved, whilst also operating under the umbrella of a reputable and established brand with all its advantages.

Kaye has been a travel agent all her adult life and had progressed up to management level in her last corporate job. She had always enjoyed interacting with clients the most, but this was something she found lacking in her managerial role. Kaye became unhappy in her position because it had "become too directional, focusing on management and sales targets".

Whilst still in her job, she was aware of a local woman whose success as an independent travel agent had made her a bit of a legend within the travel industry. This woman was a franchisee of a firm called Travel Counsellors. So when Kaye was made redundant, she didn't need to look too far for inspiration.

Kaye recalls the time when she was invited to the office of the woman whose success had so inspired her. "I was swept away by the calmness of her office environment," remembers Kaye.

A new way to do the job Kaye loved

The franchise owner, Travel Counsellors, has been in business for over 20 years and specialises in personally tailored holidays and business travel. Kaye's long experience in the industry made her a very attractive franchisee.

Barely a month after she had set out her stall as a Travel Counsellor, Kaye fell seriously ill while holidaying in Spain. Although she was lying in a hospital bed, it did not prevent her from following up on the few inquiries she had been working on before her illness. This was a stressful time for her, but she took comfort in the knowledge that she could run her business entirely from home.

There are people who enjoy researching their holidays, but not many who are comfortable doing all of their own bookings. There are also real concerns over security and financial protection (in the event of airlines or travel companies going bust) and a growing frustration at the complete lack of the personal touch that booking online involves. Especially when the customer is time poor or wants to ensure that nothing goes wrong with their travel or holiday plans. Kaye offers her customers a personalised service whilst having the buying power of her parent company.

Kaye's first year as a franchisee was an unusual one due to her illness. But she got a lot of help from head office and found there was a real support network that helped her to get to grips with a number of business-related aspects she was less familiar with, such as technology, accounts and tax.

The challenge of becoming a business owner

Her own long experience in the travel industry meant that she had extensive destination knowledge, but all of that expertise did not teach her how to run a business. In Kaye's second year, she "had to put her business brain on".

In the beginning, she was generous with her time and gave advice to friends and family who would pick her brains but not always do business with her. "It had never been about making money but at some point I realised that if I don't make money, I won't be there for my clients in a year's time."

Saying no to people who were looking for free advice, so she could prioritise genuine paying customer inquiries was a trait she had to learn.

Kaye admits that there will always be clients who get her to do all the work but still go ahead and do the final booking elsewhere. "You have to be patient," she says. When her clients book with her, they get a full service that is personalised to their needs.

Kaye's is a very customer-centric business and client feedback is very important to her. She stays in contact with her clients at various points during their travels and also passes on feedback to the suppliers, including airlines and hotels. Much of her business relies on word of mouth and referrals. "I found it difficult to ask for referrals early on. But once I got comfortable asking, the business took off." She now has clients all over the world thanks to the power of referrals and social media.

Does working on your own from the confines of your home ever get lonely? "Not really," says Kaye. She is always on the phone connected to her clients or the suppliers. The relationship with other Travel Counsellors is complementary, rather than competitive. They are invited to annual conferences by the head office and there are local get-togethers too for franchisees to meet and share ideas.

It has been three years since Kaye became a Travel Counsellor. She loves her work and hopes to some day become one of the top counsellors within the franchise.

Lessons learnt and advice

"Joining a franchise is an easier way to start your own business without having to do something brand new. However, it is important that the franchise owner and the franchisee are the right fit for each other if their relationship is to be genuinely successful."

CHAPTER 9

Kelsey Skinner
– Director, Imperial
Innovations – The UK

Imperial Innovations is a firm that focuses on the commercialisation of some of the UK's best academic research. In her role as Director of Tech Ventures, Kelsey focuses on energy, materials and connected devices technologies.

Kelsey was originally from Colorado, USA. At the age of five, she knew with complete certainty that she wanted to be an astronaut, and realised the need to excel in maths and science if her wish was to come true. In the third grade, she signed up for extracurricular maths classes and found she was the only girl in the class.

In seventh grade, her teacher tried to hold her back by attempting to put her into a lower level for maths, but Kelsey's mother disagreed with this assessment and successfully got her daughter put back up a level. In sweet vindication of her mother's faith, Kelsey won the All School Math Award at the age of 18, beating all other girls and boys in a school with over 2,000 students.

Kelsey was also very athletic from a young age and played American Football. She was the only girl in the team at 12-years-old but a foot taller than all the boys, and earned the respect of her teammates through her game.

Her early upbringing, wonderfully supportive parents and love of things normally associated with boys prepared her well for the jobs she would do in her later working life. Today, she works in venture capital, one of the most male-dominated industries in the world.

When childhood dream met reality

So what happened to the dream of being an astronaut? "I was a finalist for the Rhodes scholarship and still dead set on becoming an astronaut," Kelsey tells me. "I had some phenomenal mentors along the way, two of whom were

Rhodes scholars and one of them was coaching me at the time. One of the questions from the panel was, "How will you fight the world's fight?" In trying to answer this rather profound question, Kelsey realised that, deep down, her reasons for wanting to become an astronaut had more to do with its perceived "sexiness" than because it was the best way to contribute her skills to the world.

Resetting aspirations and the role of mentors

Within a few months of this realisation, at the age of 22, Kelsey changed her graduate programme to Renewable Energy. As an engineer and scientist, she was very aware that many great technologies never become commercialised. She wanted to understand why. It had become obvious to her that this lack of success had little to do with science, and everything to do with business.

Another one of Kelsey's mentors encouraged her to go to business school in Stanford. She remembers it as "a very transitional time that in hindsight set me on the path that led me to my sweet spot". At business school, Kelsey was taken with the idea of becoming an entrepreneur or joining a start-up. "But I couldn't decide which start-up to work with – there were too many and I didn't know how to differentiate them." Instead, she went to work for a Venture Capital firm in order to learn what makes a really great start-up.

Kelsey talks a great deal about mentors and the role they played in her life's decisions. How did she find them? "I am definitely the type of person who loves learning from others," she says. Kelsey also credits her mother who "always encouraged me to get to know people better if I found them interesting". She tells me about a book called *Mindset*, by Dr Carol Dweck, which transformed the way she thought about her life. "The book is about experimentation, risk taking and feeling comfortable in failing. People who are smart growing up grow up not expecting to fail." Kelsey admits to fitting into the smart but scared category. She thinks that until she had read the book she suffered from "imposter syndrome", like some other smart women, where you worry that you are not really as smart as everyone thinks you are. The book is about figuring things out through trying and sometimes failing. Reading it was liberating for Kelsey and the book made her more comfortable to "put herself out there".

Trying new things and always learning

Being willing to try new things and learn from others played a role in how she got her first job at a VC firm. Whilst she was a student at Stanford, Kelsey volunteered at conferences and events and particularly loved working at the registration desk. "I got to meet lots of really interesting people," she says. Kelsey had kept in touch with a VC investor after he gave a very interesting speech to her class at business school, and she met him again at a conference a couple of years later. The conversation led him to hire her for a role at his firm.

Kelsey did a number of internships during her student years in order to see what she liked. What advice does she have for young people who are unsure of their career path? "It is important to have a hypothesis," says Kelsey. "To this day I have a variety of hypotheses about what I want to do in life. Ask yourself these questions: what am I good at and what do

I think I want to do in life? Go talk to people who can poke holes in your thesis in a constructive way."

How does she deal with it if this openness exposes her to negativity? "I try to view it constructively and see what I can learn from it. Most of the time there's good nuggets to learn. But then sometimes people or situations are just negative. Honestly, I proactively try to keep pure negativity out of my life. Intentionality is a theme in my life," says Kelsey.

A woman in a man's world

We talk about her first job in venture capital: a million miles away from her childhood dream of being an astronaut. "I got out of research to go into business because I like people and this helped me to succeed in VC. Early stage investing is all about aligned vision. Recognising what is a realistic business plan and coming up with a deal structure that is a win-win gives me a real buzz." "That being said, it is important to recognise that VC is not the right funding solution for the vast majority of start-ups," Kelsey goes on to say.

Why are there still so few women in her industry? The number has grown in recent years, from four to six per cent, but it is still woefully low compared to even other financial services. "I'm disappointed there aren't more women. VC firms tend to be small and run like a family. There is a need for greater diversity of thought and experience. As a woman in VC, people are more likely to remember me [because we are in such a minority.] At the early stages, I am more likely to work closely with them [the investee company] and want to be in partnership."

Do women in predominantly male environments generally behave differently towards each other in the workplace? "Successful women are much more polarising than successful men. There's some great research out of Stanford's business school that shows this empirically. So I accepted that some people just won't like me, and that actually makes it easier." Cultural differences in how workplace bonding occurs are also worth noting. "In the UK, for instance, bonding between male colleagues occurs mainly by making fun of each other, and "being mean" to each other."

Kelsey thinks that women behave differently from men in the workplace, partly because of societal norms, and simply by being aware of these differences might help young women cope better in very male dominated environments.

Moving to the UK from the USA

What made Kelsey move from California to London? She was visiting the UK a few years ago and met a Brit who she fell in love with and got married to last year. The VC firm she was working with at the time sponsored her for a six-month stay in the UK, so that she could work on European entrepreneurship and investment opportunities. She used this time to network extensively.

As passionate as she is about early stage investing, she knows an important part of being a successful early stage VC is having deep pockets. This eventually led her to Imperial Innovations, the UK-based firm that specialises in the commercialisation of early stage technologies that are coming out of research within the golden triangle of UK universities – Cambridge, Imperial College and Oxford.

"Moving to the UK has been the greatest adventure of my life. London is a great place to live. The cultural differences are challenging and wearying but on the other hand, they make me grow."

Advice to young women in male-dominated industries

What factors does Kelsey think contributed to her success and can she offer any further advice to young women who may be looking to join male dominated industries? Kelsey points to some of the important breaks she enjoyed in her career. "First, the mentor who encouraged me to B-school, then getting the VC job in California and finally getting the job I am in now." In each situation, she was fortunate to have people who backed her completely. "One of the key ways to get people to like me is to ask lots of questions and be genuinely interested in what they say and think – it often challenges my own ways of thinking. The other is to offer affirmation and show gratitude. Doing little things to show people you appreciate their good work can bring lots of goodwill."

Lessons learnt and advice

- Kelsey is philosophical about many of the things she has done in the past that she now regrets. "I view them as points in my journey and feel that I probably needed to go through them at that time."

- Kelsey thinks she was so eager to prove herself in both job situations, she ended up "putting people offside by being too promoting and not humble enough".
- She remembers the advice an older female colleague who was leaving once gave her, which left a lasting impression. The advice was: "Don't worry. In the end, it always works out."

"I learn lessons every day and write them down on my phone. This helps me to constantly evolve. Put yourself out there. Everything is an experiment."

CHAPTER 10

Kiran Kandade – Founder, Socrates Learning – Singapore

Kiran's aim is to help organisations to "do well by doing good" with a focus on sustained change. Socrates Learning is the embodiment of Kiran's two decades of business experience and her core values in the field of organisational development.

Kiran's first job was as a lecturer in Physics for two years followed by a two-year stint in electronic and instrumentation manufacturing. She then moved into a career of writing software in India. Some years later, when she was married with one child, the family moved to Singapore. She went on to have two more children and successfully combined being a mother with forging a demanding career, eventually rising to the role of an executive director at the Singapore subsidiary of a French multinational firm.

In her working life, she had come to realise that her corporate success was down to her personal management style, which relied on managing change through trial and error, as well as instinct. This led to her interest in the area of Organisational Development and planted the seeds of her entrepreneurial venture that focuses on helping businesses to "do well by doing good".

The end of an era and new beginnings

In 2008, Kiran chose to end 22 years of marriage and became a single parent to her three children. She decided to quit her job as she needed to "be there for my boys" who have Becker Muscular Dystrophy. Although both her boys are fiercely independent, she needed to find a work-life balance that put their needs first. She recalls that time as liberating in many ways, but at the same time scary, because she was "leaving the only life I had ever known" – first, as a daughter living with parents, and then as a wife and mother.

Kiran's love for learning has meant that she thrives on academia. She has three Masters degrees, the first being in Physics, the second in Knowledge Engineering (Artificial Intelligence) and another in Organisational Development, and has recently embarked on a PhD. Many things about her management style are intuitive, but she realised there were things that could also be learned. Kiran believes that having the necessary academic qualifications has gained her greater credibility in the market and helped her to approach things more methodically. This will be important to her if she is to be a facilitator and a catalyst for change within organisations.

She decided to call her business Socrates Learning after the Greek philosopher who taught others by asking questions, rather than simply providing all the answers. "Asking the right questions is critical to learning", says Kiran.

Her approach relies on using the power of positivity to make a change that is visible, measurable, sustained, and transformational. This might be in areas such as gender balance at work, creativity, innovation, etc.

The early struggles

"When you no longer have the name of a big company on your business card, selling is much harder as you have to sell yourself," says Kiran. You may get a foot in the door but they may not be ready to buy from you. As a result, she found herself doing a lot of work for free in an attempt to establish credibility. But she realised that she was not only earning nothing, but also her input was not valued. Those who embraced her "free" input did not feel committed to making a sustained change, thereby diminishing the importance of it.

Although times were hard and the stress of making ends meet was intense, she had the invaluable support of her closest friends and family. Her work with local communities and not for profit organisations helped her to build credibility and meet people who had a similar mindset. In the past year or so, things finally turned around for Kiran with customers appreciating the work she does for them and being willing to pay for it.

Kiran does not see herself as an entrepreneur, but rather a collaborator and facilitator. Her heart lies in academia and she really wants to put what she has learnt on the job to the test via academic research. She also wants to expand Socrates Learning and build a collaborative network of people around the world that share her vision of helping companies to do well whilst doing good.

True to Kiran's passion for learning, despite all odds, in September this year she embarked on a PhD at ESADE Business School in Barcelona, Spain. Kiran recently told me that she is "thriving in a learning environment and loving her fourth lease at student life".

What would Kiran do differently if she had her time again? "I wish I had done more "free" work for community organisations early on [rather than companies] and had focused on collaborations from day one".

Lessons learnt and advice

- I am a firm believer in the importance of collaboration over competition. Being naturally good at networking made it relatively easy for Kiran to make connections.

- I volunteered my services to local community organisations which gave me experience, a track record and helped me build useful connections with like-minded people.
- I learnt to internalise my own teachings. It helped me to deal with my own difficult circumstances after the break-up of my marriage.

"Be willing to give something before asking for something. However hard times may be, things do eventually work out."

CHAPTER 11

Meera Dabir
– Wall Artist – India

Meera uses colours, patterns and textures to transform walls in living and workplaces. She has a huge portfolio of her bespoke past projects that demonstrate a range of complex, nuanced and sophisticated works of art.

Meera spent her childhood in Saudi Arabia, where she had minimal engagement with the local culture. She and her family were far more influenced by Western media and remained close to the Indian culture. She had wanted to study Art in Mumbai but failed a prerequisite test at high school that supposedly measured creativity and aptitude for a degree in art: a sad indictment of an educational system that values conformity over genuine creativity.

Meera always knew she would do something creative but had thought she was better with words. She took up a copywriting job but "hated it" and quit shortly afterwards. She looks back at the time when she was 21, had just graduated with a degree in Humanities and did not have a clue what she wanted to do for a career. "So I just partied," she says, completely seriously. "In hindsight, it was early networking" that put her in touch with people who may have helped her to move into what she now does for a living.

Finding her artistic niche

"India was on the cusp of globalisation and the lifestyle bubble had started to occur," Meera says, referring to the shift towards more ostentatious forms of interior design and the use of art to define people's homes and workplaces. She was living at home with her parents and would create props for photoshoots for friends, with no real consideration for money at that point. "This was just about experimenting and spreading my wings; basically my version of going to art school."

Her first real break came when she was asked to decorate the interior of a salon that was being launched by friends who were on a shoestring budget. "Again, I wasn't really thinking of money at this point because it just seemed like a fun opportunity. I hadn't really thought of what could come out of it."

Meera's artwork at the salon became an excellent advertisement for her. "I just found that one of the things I liked doing and was good at, happened to be something that people would pay me enough for me to consider it as a vocation. The first few years were intense as I did all the work myself and charged very little", recalls Meera. She considers that time to have been a fantastic learning experience.

Battling preconceptions

Her kind of art, which uses colours, textures and patterns to transform walls, was unique to her, making it hard for her and others to judge what her work was really worth. She battled with a very Indian preconception that equated physical labour with people from lower socioeconomic strata and hence being less valuable. Hers is not the sort of art that can be put on a blueprint for someone else to execute.

Meera remembers one year when she had four jobs but only two clients paid up. She also found that some clients haggled. She had not yet cottoned on to the tactic of inflating her price in anticipation of it being beaten down by people who had a lifelong haggling habit.

Meera had no mentors or people who could advise her on how to get smarter with her business tactics. Her parents were very encouraging and supportive of her, but she had to learn to fend for herself in business. "My family had tended to be in conventional jobs that they stuck with for life," Meera says by way of explanation as to why they were unable to advise her.

The commercial challenges

Her work always won her good feedback and this helped her to win new customers through their recommendations. It was one of her early clients who sat her down one day and advised her to get more structure into her business, including a Terms and Conditions page. Because of the customised nature of her work, her rates can't be compared with more standardised services. The idea was that the T&Cs would help get the money question agreed upon at the outset and so clients would know what to expect for the money they were being charged.

The problem for her still is that "90 per cent of people didn't read them." As a result, she still occasionally faces situations where the client changes their mind mid-way through a project. This results in more material needing to be bought and more time spent, which escalates the overall cost of the project. And yet when it comes to settling the bill, there is sometimes resistance over the extra costs.

The commercial aspect of her work is the one area that Meera struggles with most. She knows she is not alone, most creative people are not very good at making money from their art during their lifetime. The other thing about her kind of art is that it is a challenge to scale up, as each job is unique and she can only work on one job at any one time. It is also difficult to expand geographically because she has to be present for every job, which unfortunately adds to the overall cost of the project.

Could Meera train others so they could work with her? She thinks not. "The range of services I offer is so vast that no matter how much I train people, there are some things only I can do."

She has a knack of reading colours in a way that most people can't, and it is these nuanced colours and the way she mixes them that gives her finished work its uniqueness. She works closely with her clients so that their personality and tastes are reflected in her art. She now has a huge portfolio of her past projects, including samples that demonstrate a range of complex, nuanced, sophisticated and interesting artwork.

For Meera, her art is less about the money (even if that is really important, given it is how she earns a living) and all about her client. "It is about making them happy. It is expressed through me, but it belongs to them. There is honesty to the intention, as I am doing bespoke work for them." She goes on to explain why it is quite different from other kinds of art forms that can be displayed or sold. "When creating a canvas you create it for yourself. If it speaks to the people who see it, then they will buy it". Meera sees her role as that of an interpreter who turns her client's vision and tastes into a work of art in their own living space.

Has she considered collaborating with others in the value chain? Meera does work with some interior designers, occasionally on the request of a client. There is something very down to earth about her approach. She says she can't relate to some people in the interior designing industry who tend to be very luxury biased, and finds their "tyranny of design" off-putting.

Despite her success and the fact that her work is more widely recognised than she is, Meera knows that she needs to find a way to make her business more repeatable for herself. Not least because her work is so sustainable and durable that it lasts 10-15 years before a client may need to come back for a replacement!

Lessons learnt and advice

- "Work to please yourself first. My work only goes to the clients for feedback once I'm happy with its quality. They can tweak to adjust it to their specific tastes, but only once I'm satisfied with it."
- "If you're starting out, first work with someone established, even if the work isn't what you want to do. You need to learn how to operate in a professional environment without having to shoulder the entire burden of the mistakes you will inevitably make."
- "Respect your clients. Everything you will ever create, ever learn, ever achieve is due to them affording you the opportunity."
- "Don't let your clients disrespect you. There will always be people who don't see the point of your

work. They're entitled to their opinion but that in no way means your work is irrelevant or lacks value."

- "Plan your finances. Be smart. Save. Invest. Build a nest egg. It'll give you the freedom to say no to jobs that don't interest you."
- "If the hoops you have to jump through to get the project are becoming increasingly narrower, sometimes it's best to let the job go. You never lose out on what's inevitably coming to you."

"Chase growth not the money. Chase what's new, what excites you and engages you. That will ensure that your work will remain relevant. Chasing money is chasing safety and no one ever created anything of value chasing safety."

CHAPTER 12

Mimi Saigal
– Dancer &
Choreographer – India

Mimi is a trained Indian classical dancer with 25 years of experience working as a professional dancer and choreographer, creating and teaching unique Bollywood dance sequences at Indian weddings.

Mimi grew up in a Bengali family in India where learning an art form in one's formative years was considered very important. Mimi's mother enrolled her into (a classical form of Indian dance) *Bharatnatyam* classes from the age of five. "I always enjoyed dance and because I was never forced to do it, I became a natural at it," says Mimi.

Her talent and commitment to dance was only accentuated by the opportunity to learn from the masters of her time. In Delhi, she was fortunate to count India's famous classical dancers Sonal Mansingh and Rohinton Cama as her gurus.

When she moved to Mumbai to complete her university education, she stayed involved in dance by going along to various dance shows, especially during religious festivals like *Durga Puja*. Even as she successfully performed in her (the debut performance of a *Bharatnatyam* student) *Arangetram* she was also interested in a lighter form of dance as seen in Bollywood movies.

Bollywood beckons

Mimi had trained as an Interior Designer but the lure of dance was never far away. She started working with a renowned dancer and choreographer who is credited with some of the most memorable and mesmerising dance sequences in Bollywood history.

Mimi's vivacious personality helped her to fit in with a group who were mostly women and came from varied backgrounds, with dance being the one common factor. She learnt early on that this was a highly emotive industry with envy and even outright jealousy, never far from the minds of those who worked in it. Mimi was relied on to do a lot of the marketing and smooth ruffled feathers because of her good communication skills. Looking back on that time she admits that although she really longed to do more choreography, the eight years she spent working in Bollywood and the experience of dealing with different kinds of people proved invaluable to her in later life.

Motherhood and finding a new niche

When Mimi had her first child, she took a five-year break during which she had her second child and kept her interest in dance alive by teaching students in a local Bengali school. "Dance was like breathing and it was very easy to come back to," says Mimi. She considers herself to be very fortunate to have always had the unconditional support of her husband and in-laws.

Mimi had decided not to go back to Bollywood and found she could not return to Interior Designing either because she had been out of it for too long. As a result, she had lost contact with suppliers and the latest market trends.

It was around this time that a new trend was taking hold on the Indian wedding scene: the explosive arrival of a very organised and choreographed *"Sangeet"* wherein various members of the family, from the bride's or the groom's side, put on a dance show for other wedding guests. But there is seasonality to weddings and Mimi could only take on a limited number of clients at any one time. In the quiet times, she continued to teach dance in schools.

What is it like working with a different family every time? "Choreography is not just about dance", says Mimi. "People sometimes just look at the price [as a deciding factor]. Dance is physical and the person who comes into your house should be a positive person who acts as a bridge between the various members of the family. You need to understand the undercurrents". It takes Mimi "about ten minutes" to determine the nature of these "undercurrents" so that she can focus on those who are unhappy. On many occasions, Mimi finds she has to "work with the head of someone who may have never danced". She also acts as compere for the show. With her years of experience and naturally bubbly personality, she is able to put everyone at ease, even those who might be at first unwilling to dance.

Competition, customisation and client satisfaction

Mimi has been a professional choreographer for dances at Indian weddings for 15 years. She has loved every job she has ever done and the satisfactions she gets, especially seeing someone who has never danced before go up on stage and perform, far outweighs the money she earns.

Despite her excellent reputation and customers coming to her through word of mouth, she admits that every season the work gets tougher. "There is a lot of talent and competition, and the market is opening up with customers having more options," she says. "You constantly have to market yourself," a task she is not entirely comfortable with. The nature of her work means that she gets repeat business from families who have others sons and daughters to be married off. Guests at weddings who like her work are also a natural target market for future custom.

Mimi's hands-on approach, customised choreography, attention to detail, relentless enthusiasm to get every member of the family dancing comfortably, and her years of experience all translate into a price tag that is higher than some of her competitors' fees.

Mimi does not have a standard pricing formula. What she charges varies, depending on a number of criteria, which includes the financial situation of her clients. She always aims to talk at length with the family to understand what they want from their choreographer and how much they are willing to spend. She understands that one price does not fit all and does not see the need to compete on price.

She uses assistants who are freelance dancers and help out as and when there is work. She ensures that at least they are paid on time and as agreed. She admits that she is lucky that she can choose "not to compromise her talent and has never had to scrap for money".

Mimi's Unique Selling Proposition (USP)

Mimi believes her forte is teaching age appropriate dance to women over 30. "Being a good dancer does not necessarily mean you are a good choreographer or a good teacher. It is also not about me, it is about making the client look good."

Mimi has a story about a lady who didn't want to dance. The rest of the family really wanted her to take part in it but they could not get her to agree. The woman eventually confided in Mimi that she was very self-conscious about her upper arms. So Mimi created a choreography that involved her never having to raise her arms during the entire dance sequence. It is such attention to detail that wins Mimi repeat business and recommendations from happy clients.

Mimi sees her business as a labour of love and is motivated by much more than just money. She admits that she is lucky to be in a position where she has a very supportive husband who is also the main breadwinner in the family. His support is crucial in doing a job that is not 9 to 5 and involves working evenings and weekends.

The importance of innovation and word of mouth

Mimi is passionate about the need to innovate. "Talent is recognised but you need to sustain it and constantly innovate. Each job is a platform for the next job, so you can never sit back. I want my work to speak for me as I don't do any marketing."

Mimi tells me that she has never used her choreography more than once, even if it is for the same song. "Everything gets copied and it is getting very competitive. So I have to innovate all the time." She is very aware that a dance at a wedding can be videoed and put on YouTube for anyone to reproduce. She believes her clients pay her to get something fresh that has never been seen before.

Lessons learnt and advice

- "Art is more about the heart than the mind. Be passionate, don't do it just for the money."
- "Find out for yourself what makes you different."
- "Believe in yourself, but test your skill in the real world to find out if you are ready for others who may try to break you down."
- "Innovate and be willing to learn from others. "
- "Make friends and collaborate with others who may have the skills you don't have."
- "When you do make money, spend it wisely, and if possible invest it for a time in the future when you might not have any."
- "Stay humble."

"Talent alone is not enough. You need to be a combination of a number of things, including patience and the ability to discuss money clearly and calmly."

CHAPTER 13

Nikhita Kapur and Pooja Kapur Co-Founders, Designiks – India

Designiks is the result of Nikhita's, passion for designing tasteful traditional Indian outerwear whilst, where possible and practical, engaging the skills of those who are autistic, blind or victims of brutality to help empower them. She has only just finished senior school and is due to start her university education. Her mother Pooja is her support and mentor.

This is Nikhita's story as told by her mother Pooja, without whose guidance and support Designiks could not exist.

Pooja's older teenage daughter Nikhita loves fashion and enjoys art as a hobby. Nikhita, apart from being academically gifted and artistic, is also a keen sportswoman. On one occasion, about three years ago, she was due to travel to Sweden to play football with her school and needed to carry a traditional Indian outfit to wear at the opening ceremony. A trip to the local shopping mall proved disappointing; there was nothing she liked in the affordable price range and the designer wear was too expensive for a 15-year-old to wear.

The moment of inspiration

Nikhita had spotted a gap in the market for young women like her: modern yet tasteful traditional Indian clothes at an affordable price. She decided she wanted to try her hand at designing clothes that she would be happy to wear and with this idea Designiks was born.

In most modern cities like Mumbai, dressing up in elaborate traditional Indian clothes tends to be reserved for special occasions like weddings. Nikhita's very first collection was driven by the kinds of designs she would want to wear in terms of colours, fabrics and style. It was a steep learning curve for her and so at first she relied heavily on her mother on matters, such as buying the right kind of fabric and getting it made as per her design. It came as a pleasant surprise to both mother and daughter how aligned their thinking was and how quickly Nikhita picked up some of the business basics.

This was all taking place even as Nikhita had to contend with schoolwork, house captaincy and preparation for important exams. They didn't want Designiks to get in the way of Nikhita's studies and so she permitted herself only one day a week to focus on the creative aspect of the business whilst Pooja would do the sourcing of fabric, and getting them made by high-quality and reliable seamstresses and tailors. It was not long before Nikhita had learnt the ropes and was getting involved in those aspects of the business too.

Exploring the niche

How did they know they were on the right track and that customers would be interested in buying their designs? "Nikhita was very particular about not getting external input on their designs in the early stages," says Pooja. Nikhita wanted to explore their niche unhindered and come up with something that was original. She feared that feedback at that stage would be based on people's own choices or what other designers were creating. Nikhita also avoided selling to friends whose feedback she feared would be biased, largely by their effort to encourage and support her.

Over the course of the second half of 2014, Designiks steadily built up a collection of about 15 outfits that were showcased for the first time using Facebook. The feedback and positive comments that came from complete strangers confirmed to them that they were on to something good. The page went viral and soon they were getting requests from women around the world wanting Designiks to physically showcase their outfits with a view to selling them.

This posed a dilemma for Pooja, who did not want to "make a business out of a 16-year-old," but wanted to help build something towards her future. They were overwhelmed by the positive feedback they were getting, as well as the repeat inquiries from interested buyers. Pooja sensed that the business had already gone further than they had planned.

So they announced that they would be taking an extended break of six to nine months to let Nikhita focus on her schoolwork. Despite this, they still received firm orders and found themselves selling 70 outfits in the short space of time that Nikhita was able to devote to the business during her school holidays.

Managing customer expectations whilst 'doing good'

Pooja is keen to point out that the fabric and other raw material that go into the creation of each outfit are of the highest quality, as is the handiwork that brings Nikhita's designs to life. Although Nikhita's original idea was to create affordable traditional wear for young women like herself, the outfits they create sell at premium prices and are designed for special occasions, such as weddings. "We need to ensure the quality of the garment is commensurate with the price and the expectations of the customer who is buying," says Pooja

But there is more to Designiks than exquisite designer-wear. Designiks Creates is a pet project of Nikhita, who gets "special people" to work on embellishing accessories like scarves, clothes hangers and create things like cushion covers, table mats, coasters and other items of homeware. These are clearly labelled so that the buyer can see which NGO has helped to create them.

Nikhita's vision: a business with a heart

The appeal of Designiks lies not just in the stunningly elegant designs, but it is the work that the business does with disadvantaged people that lies at the core of the enterprise. Pooja's commitment to helping disadvantaged people earn a living has been passed down to her daughter, and you will read about Pooja's story and her initiative, Towards a Special Cause (TASC), later in this book.

Designiks aims to support their chosen NGOs by sourcing products from them that complement their own creations. These often tend to be accessories or packaging material or decorated hangers that can be sold alongside much higher value outfits.

They have also come up with ideas for new products that are made by people in disadvantaged communities, including those with autism, vision impairment and women who have been victims of abuse. In the longer term, Pooja and Nikhita see Designiks Support as an initiative that will create jobs for NGOs with skilled resources.

This is a long-term vision and needs to be handled with care. Unfortunately, people often associate the work produced by NGOs as cheap labour and not of the best quality. Pooja is acutely aware that this perception would not sit well with a premium priced product. However, for lower-priced items, such as the accessories, she sees ample room for NGO participation.

Much of Designiks' early success is down to attention to detail, product quality and ensuring that the customer is happy with their purchase. Pooja admits that they have spent "way more than they have earned" but is happy they are building strong foundations for Nikhita's future.

Helping a number of "special" people to become productive members of society, whilst pursuing her passion through Designiks makes Nikhita the fresh face of responsible capitalism.

Lessons learnt and advice

These are Nikhita's words:

- "I've learnt how an idea, a design or concept is the easiest part of creating a product."
- "As a small two-member team, we've had no one to delegate any responsibility to. This has helped us to learn so much, including:
  - □ The importance of detail and quality in a finished product.
  - □ The intricacies of fits and measurements.
  - □ Multi-tasking
  - □ Time management and client deadlines.
  - □ Viablity of the design beyond merely 'the look of it'.

□ The nearly 20 different components from fabric to embellishments for each design and the effort it takes to procure them.

□ Budget and pricing."

"In our pursuit to do good through our business, we need to be careful about the negative perception of getting things made by NGOs. We need to raise awareness and find a way to manage customer expectations."

CHAPTER 14

Tia Moin
– Human Resources
Consultant – The UK

Tia is a freelance organisational psychologist who analyses psychometric test results on behalf of corporate clients as a part of their recruitment process. She is based in the UK but currently serves the Australian market.

Tia was born and brought up in England. After completing a degree in Psychology, her very first job involved telesales, selling the firm's HR software to corporate clients. She had not expected to work in sales and felt her qualifications as a psychologist were not being used in the role. However, Tia took to the task with clinical professionalism, treating it as a numbers game. She moved from call to call, recognising quickly if there was going to be a sale and moving on swiftly if not.

To her surprise, this approach worked well and she found she was more successful than some of her colleagues who spent time on each call, trying to persuade the reluctant person at the other end to buy. The sales skills she developed in this first role served her well in later life.

Tia recalls advice from one of her early managers that always stuck in her memory. He told her once, "Never leave a job until you have completely mastered it, and you feel you have nothing more to learn from it." She eventually networked her way into an actual HR role at the accounting and consultancy firm Arthur Anderson, where she worked as an HR representative for one of their regional offices.

Tia believes she straddles what she calls generations X and Y. The former spent long periods of time in the same job, whilst the latter tend to move from job to job more frequently. When she started at Arthur Anderson in her ideal job, she thought it would be for life. But that was not to be and the firm's troubles post-Enron crisis meant that she was made redundant.

Turning a crisis into an opportunity

Although she lost her dream job, Tia chose to turn a crisis into an opportunity. She utilised her career transition programme to relocate to Australia; living and working abroad was something she'd always wanted to do. While in Australia, she got married and decided to live there permanently.

The HR industry in Australia differed markedly from the UK, and she found herself being more attracted to a role of an Organisational Psychologist, which was still within the HR field but its approach had a more scientific grounding. As a result, she decided to study a postgraduate psychology qualification that required some clinical psychology experience. It involved dealing with people who had been traumatised in some way or needed therapy for psychological disorders and mental illnesses.

Tia soon discovered that she was not suited to this type of work. "It takes a certain kind of resilience to work in clinical psychology, the pressure of dealing with life or death situations started to wear me down. I found it much more appealing to work in the field of Organisational Psychology to help people enhance their performance."

Once she had achieved her qualification, she continued to gain experience in HR, specifically within her chosen area of specialisation. This primarily involved a psychological assessment of candidates applying for jobs, as well as the assessment of individuals, teams and leaders for coaching and development to help organisations achieve their performance goals.

Discovering her niche and motherhood

Tia realised she had found her niche in this field. She had been working for the same firm for six years, rising up to the Head of the Delivery Team, and had reached a stage in life when she wanted to start a family. Tia loved her job: it was fast-paced, challenging and she had built a team up from the ground. She recruited and trained new staff members and put in long hours to ensure that client demands were met. Working in a consulting firm is not the usual 9 to 5 job, and she had put off having children for as long as possible to ensure that she had established herself in her career first. She often invested additional hours and effort into the role to ensure that she achieved this.

Tia had a baby boy and after returning from maternity leave, asked her employer if she could go back to her old job on a part-time basis. Childcare facilities were sparse in Sydney and going back to full-time work was not an option. She was disappointed to find that her former employer was not able to offer her the flexibility she needed.

Although Tia returned, she did not stay for long and was offered a role at another assessment firm that was happy for her to work flexibly on a part-time basis. Her manager was a woman who understood the challenges of being a working mum and showed the flexibility that was needed to leverage Tia's skills, qualifications and experience in an appropriate role.

Heartbreak and upheaval

When Tia's son was only two years old, her marriage broke down and she made the difficult decision to move back to England. It all happened so fast that all she could do was focus on survival and her son's best interests, and so did not think about work or a potential source of income at the time. Tia admits that she was lucky, as she had her mother's home to go to, and she was not as financially insecure as some others in her position are.

The benefits of networking and globalisation

Before she left Australia she had been encouraged by her manager to set up as a contractor. "The field of organisational psychology is a niche area that tends to be female dominated, in Australia at least. Once these women have children, many drop out of consulting firms because they tend not to be very family friendly, and end up working on a contract basis – a flexible, part-time option that works for both the organisation and the women who have children." Tia was grateful for this parting advice, as it was both easy to set up and a saving grace in terms of income once she had moved to the UK.

The contacts she made whilst in Australia helped her to set up a freelance business from home, thanks to the Internet. The time difference between the UK and Australia also helps. She works as an "overflow option", filling in when there is more work that can be done by her client's full-time workforce. As the UK was waking up and Australia was winding down for the day, Tia would complete work 'overnight' for her Australian clients.

"Every role I've ever done, I have given it a proper go," she says. Tia is now at a juncture where she does not have to worry about the volume of work, or indeed whether she is earning enough to take care of herself and her son. But she does yearn for a more challenging opportunity to do more than just analyse the results of the psychological tests. Fortunately, she is able to do this in the knowledge that her skills and experience are in demand, whether she chooses to work on a flexible, contract basis or in a more permanent role within an organisation. She believes that is down to a good work ethic and establishing excellent connections.

Lessons learnt and advice:

- "Don't leave a job until you've mastered it, learning new skills is never a waste and at some point, they will come in handy, even if you can't see it yet."
- "Recognise the importance of networking as early on as possible in your career. Never burn any bridges; the network I rely on for my business was built over many years and I met some of my contacts when I was a 'rookie' in the industry."
- "Look for the silver lining/opportunity in every situation. Being made redundant opened the path for me to try living and working abroad in Australia. My marriage breaking down and my decision to relocate to the UK paved a path for me to set up as an independent consultant, so that I could balance work

and family more easily, and ultimately, as a result, I have spent more time with my son."

"Recognise your own worth as a working mother, even if the company that you work for doesn't. I had to find another employer that did appreciate my worth and that was prepared to be flexible to leverage my skills and talents."

CHAPTER 15

Vandana Patel – Superintendent Pharmacist, Medimpo – The UK

Vandana harnessed her passion for science by choosing to become a pharmacist. Medimpo is a family-run chain of nine pharmacies in the South East of England that Vandana helped build up over more than three decades, making many personal sacrifices along the way.

Vandana grew up in Zimbabwe, but her family originally came from India. When it came to education she remembers her mother being her main source of inspiration. Despite her mother's lack of formal schooling, she wanted to see all her children get a good education.

When it was time for Vandana to pick her subjects for university, her school tried to dampen her ambitions and suggested that she go into laboratory testing, rather than medicine. She admits that becoming a doctor in Zimbabwe was not an option she had seriously considered because of the inhospitable working conditions and long hours it entailed.

Vandana's older brother, who was studying in the UK at that time, wrote to her urging her to consider going to university for a degree in pharmacy. Given that she loved the sciences, particularly biology and chemistry, this seemed like a natural progression to her. She joined the School of Pharmacy for a degree course in Zimbabwe. The course got more interesting and engaging as she went into the second and third year, largely because it involved greater interaction with medics, hospital wards and consultants.

A life-changing move to the UK

After graduation and her pre-registration training in hospital, Vandana decided to move to the UK for a reciprocal registration. Once in the UK, she did a Masters in Pharmacy at Chelsea College (now part of Kings College London) for which she got a grant from the Zimbabwean government. After completing her Masters and her registration as a pharmacist, she started working with Moss Chemists as a community pharmacist. It was at this time that she met Kiran, who went on to become her husband. Within six months of her marriage in 1984, Vandana's husband's family had acquired their first pharmacy, followed by a second one a year later.

Was it daunting to go from being a recently qualified pharmacist to jointly running a pharmacy? "It was frightening at first, but at the same time, I was not daunted. There was this great urge to improve oneself and do well. So sometimes I worked seven days a week". A strong work ethic is in their DNA as "both sets of parents were hard working, but not professionals," says Vandana.

In 1990 they added a third pharmacy to their stable and 12 years later purchased a fourth one. In 2003, they acquired a pharmacy business that comprised three pharmacies and had a bigger turnover than their own business had at the time. Today Medimpo continues to successfully run its portfolio of nine pharmacies located in South East England.

Vandana and her brother-in-law enjoyed a good working relationship with complementary skills. He took care of the business side of things whilst Vandana was the pharmacist. "The learning curve was steep. I felt a responsibility to be a good pharmacist and to offer a good service," recalls Vandana. He was the lead on acquisitions whilst she had to step up to the plate as a "superintendent", always striving to do her best.

Balancing motherhood with career

How did Vandana cope when her children came along? "It was tough. I still had to run a household. You are kind of carried on a treadmill." Vandana had a childminder for her young children, as well as help from members of the family. "The pharmacist has to be on the premises for the pharmacy to function." Working from home or having flexible working hours was out of the question, especially when it is your own business. There was also a shortage of pharmacists at the time her children were young. "I was probably dragon woman," says Vandana with a laugh. "There were chores that needed doing" and her only day off in the week was spent doing them and getting the children to help out.

Life partner also becomes business partner

In 2005, her husband Kiran left his corporate job as an engineer to join the business. "He could see I was under a lot of pressure working on seven pharmacies," says Vandana. In time, her brother-in-law handed over the operational side of the business to Kiran. "In 2005-6, I did a part-time Diploma in Community Pharmacy at Kings College and I completed this in 2007. Returning to study in a new environment after being out of the educational field for so long was wonderful, thrilling, exciting and taught me new IT skills that I would never otherwise have learnt."

Today, the business has evolved and become more centralised with its own HR team. "My role is now more managerial and the pressures are different", says Vandana. She admits to missing the personal interaction of being a community pharmacist, but thrives in the knowledge that she has a good and loyal team of pharmacists working in the business.

Keeping an eye on the evolving landscape for pharmacies in the UK and the changing regulations also keeps Vandana occupied.

Looking back on her 32 years in the business and what she has learnt and achieved, she thinks her mother would have been proud of her. But there is also regret: "I used to feel sad that I wasn't there for my children," says Vandana. She takes some comfort in the knowledge that her children were not particularly scarred by her absence, and tells me of the time she was shown an essay written by her daughter at school in which she described Vandana as an 'inspiration'.

Personal vision for the future

"I've always wanted to write the history of my family members who went to Africa," says Vandana. She hopes she can do this and leave it as a legacy for her children and grandchildren who will never know the Zimbabwe she grew up in. "I also have lots of books I want to read," she says, before talking about her plans to find creative ways of extending the life of old *sarees*. She says she would also love to take a sabbatical from the business. "I feel I need the space to refresh and come back."

If she had her time again, would Vandana change anything? "When I look back on what I am now, I see myself as in a slow process of being developed and moulded over time. If I had to change anything, I would want to be more assertive and have greater belief in my ability to do things. I would take more time out. The sense of duty towards the business made me continue to put that first."

Lessons learnt and advice

"Life is very precious, live it fully, in whatever way is right for you."

Entrepreneurship: Finding and growing your business niche

Some of the best business ideas are born out of an unmet need. It must be a need that is experienced by others too if it is to be potentially commercial. Lifestyle changes, the emergence of new business models and technological progress are all drivers that create new demands that did not previously exist. These in turn present opportunities to offer services or products that previously had no real market. Recognising these trends early on and understanding how you can create a business from them is the starting point for any entrepreneur.

Entrepreneurship in its truest sense is all about risk taking and innovation, and it is aimed towards achieving a finite objective, whatever that might be. Does it matter if it does not always result in a scaled up, fast-growing business that employs others and creates wealth?

The women in the previous section have also successfully nurtured a business niche, embracing both risk and innovation. What differentiates them is that they each followed a career path that stemmed from a childhood passion or an early academic choice.

The women in this section all experienced a career hiatus and then found a gap in the market that they went on to fill in their own inimitable ways. Some of the businesses you will read about are in their relative infancy and we can follow their progress in the coming years with interest. A few others are finding their stride and now going from strength to strength. Two of our stories relate to businesses that started small, then grew well beyond their founders' expectations and were eventually sold to a larger competitor for a good price.

This section perhaps relates most closely to the traditional definition of start-ups that are run by entrepreneurs with ambitions that go beyond a lifestyle choice or a source of income replacement.

I have listed below some of the important things that entrepreneurs need to consider and follow if their business is to grow and create wealth for themselves and others:

- **The "A-ha!" moment**: What is your business idea? It may grow on you over time or hit you out of nowhere like a thunderbolt.
- **Market Research**: Does the idea make sense in a wider market context? Is anyone else doing it and if so, how is your idea different?
- **Customers**: Who will buy from you and why? Do you have a mechanism to get feedback from customers? What will you do with the feedback?
- **Pricing**: How will you determine what to charge for your products or services? Do you want to undercut the competition or charge a premium because you offer something far superior? Or is your offering so unique there is no price comparison available?
- **Marketing**: How will you let customers know who you are, what products you are selling and how they can buy from you? Are you going to advertise, or will you rely on other, cheaper ways to get your message out there, such as social media and word of mouth?
- **Team structure**: Will you go it alone, find a partner or have multiple owners or create a franchise model? What will your role be, and do you feel you are right for it?

- **Fulfilment**: Do you have the right team of people and the required infrastructure to ensure that you can fulfil the promise you are making to customers? Who are your suppliers and how will you deal with them? What about other stakeholders that can influence your business, such as your employees, local communities, not for profit organisations, the regulators and the government?
- **Competition**: Whom are you competing with and what is your attitude towards your competitors? How do you differ from them?
- **Financials**: What are your costs, revenues, profit margins and cash flow dynamics? Are you self-funded or do you need funding? If so, what are your choices? If you can't make money, your business has no future.
- **Vision and Culture**: Where do you see your business in the near and distant future? What is your business identity and corporate culture? Do you have an exit plan?

There are a number of additional things that go into running a successful business. How you cope with setbacks, whom you turn to for advice and support, and how you ensure you don't become too blinkered, and so lose sight of the big picture, are all important considerations.

A business is a microcosm of life itself. It needs to have a purpose, a reason for existing and a leader who will take it forward. It needs people with complementary skills if it is to succeed. How business is conducted and the tactics it deploys are often a guide to the way those who run it behave in their own lives. So when you choose a place to work, it makes sense to find out beforehand what kind of entity you will be employed by. There are not many things worse than waking up each day to work with people with whom you have nothing in common, or whose principles are in stark contrast to your own.

We can't all be leaders and nor should we seek to be. Leadership can be situation specific. You may be the boss in your workplace, but once you get home you may prefer to let someone else take on that role. Some people are born leaders, whilst others acquire the confidence to lead over time. But whether or not you were born to lead, there are no shortcuts to earning the respect of those who follow you.

Leading is about more than just being the boss and making all the decisions. It is about recognising your own strengths and weaknesses, identifying others who can fill gaps where you are found wanting, delegating responsibility, nurturing talent, and in some cases, building a long-term legacy. Good leadership is about effective communication, engendering loyalty and building a sustainable business that treats all its stakeholders with respect.

Entrepreneurship can be lonely when things go wrong. But there is nothing more rewarding than picking yourself up, learning from your mistakes, turning things around and making them right.

CHAPTER 16

Amrita Singh and Bindu Bhinde – Co-Founders, TLC – India

Amrita and Bindu started The Little Company, a professional childcare company that they successfully nurtured and grew over a 13-year period before selling it to a competitor.

Amrita and Bindu were friends long before they decided to go into business together. Amrita's first job on the completion of an MBA was to work in corporate communications at the EXIM Bank in India. From there she changed course to join a friend who had her own home furnishings business, making and exporting goods worldwide. She loved the work and enjoyed the travel that came with it.

Bindu qualified as a Chemical Engineer from BITS Pilani. She spent eight years working for Bharat Petroleum "in a very technical role". It was not a job that she particularly enjoyed but it suited her in many other ways.

The A-ha! moment

In 2001, both Amrita and Bindu were pregnant, each with their first child. Bindu decided motherhood was the perfect time to quit her job and become a full-time mum, at least until she had figured out what to do next. Amrita tells me how, like a number of Indian career women, she had hoped her parents or in-laws would be at hand to help with the baby, so that she could go back to work as before. That was not to be, as both sets of grandparents had busy lives themselves and were not free to provide the kind of full-time childcare she needed if she was to go back to work.

Once Amrita and Bindu had given birth to their children, they found their options were limited by the fact that there was no professional childcare available. Neither was content to just stay at home, especially as both had enjoyed successful corporate careers until then. They realised that they were not alone; most women found themselves unable to go back to work unless they had full-time support from close family.

The provision of professional and good quality childcare for mothers who worked or just wanted a break was very limited in India. The seeds of entrepreneurship that had been sown some years ago in Amrita's mind now blossomed into the idea of The Little Company, a childcare facility for working mothers.

Market Research

Amrita and Bindu travelled to a number of Indian cities, as well as Singapore and the UK, to learn how childcare was done on a professional basis. They informally spoke to friends and family, especially mothers with young children who had previously worked, to gauge interest. The response was very encouraging and they decided to go ahead and set up a daycare facility.

They acquired premises and some fittings from a woman who had been running a daycare centre but wanted to move on to something else. The two played to their respective strengths, dividing up the responsibilities so that Amrita, the more outgoing one of the two, took on the marketing and business development role, whilst Bindu got herself qualifications in childcare management and assumed the operational responsibilities.

When their children's daycare centre opened, they had exactly three children in their care – two of which were their own! The friends and family who had been so supportive of the idea did not go as far as sending their own children to be cared for at the facility. It was an early lesson that you cannot rely on friends and family to get your business going.

Marketing on a shoestring budget

Despite having just one paying customer, they knew there was vast unmet demand for the kind of service they were offering. They simply needed to get the message out there and ensure they could offer the best possible care, so eventually word of mouth would bring in new customers.

Amrita would stand at traffic lights and in parks in Mumbai: places where there would be mothers with their young children. She would hand out leaflets and talk to mothers about TLC. She also regularly attended seminars and conferences, where aside from it being an opportunity to learn and network, she would ask questions in order to introduce herself and make people in the audience aware of TLC.

The daycare centre became a place where mums (not just those whose were customers) could come and talk about their concerns and share stories with other mothers. Amrita and Bindu regularly invited experts to talk on specific subjects that related to mothers' or children's health and wellbeing. These were all offered for free and to anyone who wanted to attend.

Before long, TLC began to be viewed as thought leaders with regular write-ups, despite spending hardly anything at all on advertising or public relations. The goodwill and awareness they had created by offering mothers an opportunity to communicate with other mothers, long before the Internet and rise of social media, translated into inquiries and paying customers.

Initial funding and investment

Amrita and Bindu started the business with their own savings, all of which went into building the infrastructure of the first daycare centre. The day-to-day finances were managed like they would their own household budget. They focused their spending on things that really mattered: employees, training and a level of care they would want for their own children.

The equipment available in India was not of the desired quality or specifications, so they had to import the kit at a higher cost. Both were sticklers for doing things right, even if it involved a greater initial investment. Everything was clearly documented and operational processes were streamlined. This attention to detail enabled them to get an ISO certification that later opened more doors, especially amongst corporate customers.

Growing up

The business was cash flow positive after the first three months. They were always careful to ensure their employees were paid on time even if it meant neither of them earned a salary in the early years. And even when they did, it was not commensurate with what it might have been had they pursued the corporate careers they had prior to motherhood. Over a 13-year period, TLC grew from just one centre to 13 and employed 180 people before it was eventually sold to a competitor firm.

What was it was like in the early years when customers were slow to come and money was tight? "Both Bindu and I had very supportive husbands who gave us the freedom to do what we needed to do for the business without worrying about the money. Bindu and I had a very clear understanding. She managed the centre and its operations; I was the communicator. And we did not feel like we were making much of a sacrifice because we would have been taking care of our children anyway."

Having their own children at the daycare centre helped Bindu and Amrita gain real insight into what was needed to cater to the growing and changing needs of the children in their care. Listening to the needs of the parents also influenced their business offering in terms of the age group of the intake and the after-school extra-curricular activities for older children.

In terms of hiring, they were very clear about what kind of person they wanted working for them. "How you train your employees and how you treat them is very important because it will show in how they come across to the children and to their parents, " says Bindu.

The most important qualities they sought in a potential employee were a willingness to learn, empathise with the children in their care and the ability to cope with a demanding schedule. They were trained in-house so that they understood the procedures and culture of the organisation.

Once the business grew to a certain size, it became necessary to put in some minimum requirements and clear recruitment procedures. The underlying vision and tone of the business that had been set by Amrita and Bindu from day one remained in place even as the business grew.

The employees of TLC loved their jobs and were fiercely loyal, even resisting attempts by some parents to poach them. In the early days, when they were just starting out, Amrita and Bindu employed other mothers who wanted to work in a place where their child could also be taken care of. The women who worked for TLC felt empowered by being able to work in an environment that felt natural and safe to them. In some cases, this was their first experience of earning an independent living.

Having a mentor within the business, someone who had seen it all before and loved working with children also helped. Bindu tells me about Meera Khurana, a lady they had been introduced to at the very beginning of their business venture. She already had almost 30 years of experience, as well as working in childcare and had a background in psychology. She joined TLC in their second year and played a major role in the design of the curriculum. Affectionately referred to as Mother Hen, Meera was instrumental in reinforcing the need for everyone working in their daycare centres to follow strong value systems. Even after the sale of TLC, she has continued to work with the organisation providing welcome continuity.

Pricing of services

How did they decide what the right price to charge was when no real benchmark price for this service existed in the Indian market? "In the early days we would charge as much as it would cost us to pay for the staff who worked for us," recalls Amrita.

Three years into the business they had come to realise that they were grossly undercharging for their services. Increasing prices was a necessary move if they were to make a profit, so that the money could be invested back into growing the business. They decided to put an increase that in effect meant prices would double overnight. To their pleasant surprise, not a single parent left, which was a clear indication of how much they valued what TLC was doing for them.

Customer Satisfaction and Feedback

The partnership with parents is another key building block to running a successful daycare centre. TLC had an open door policy for parents, which meant they were welcome to visit any time they wanted. Mothers' Club on weekends was a forum for mums to come together, share experiences and make suggestions. For instance, one of the mums asked if they could create a daily report of each child's activities. They willingly embraced this at first, but soon discovered it was a lot of work and quite a challenge to find teachers who could express themselves in good written English. The initiative remained but they reduced the frequency of reporting to once a quarter. Bindu remembers how much parents and other extended family cherished these reports that beautifully laid out their child's progress over time.

Bindu also recalls occasions when family members, often the grandparent of a child in their care, would come along and spend time with the children at the daycare centre. It was a lovely initiative that made them feel closer to their grandchild's life and provided an opportunity for them to share a talent with the children, such as telling a story or singing.

The beginning of the end

They were in their fourth year when Bindu made the difficult decision to move to London and accompany her husband, whose job was taking him there. At this point, the centre was thriving with about 70 children in their care and about 15 women who were employed by them. They had also just won a contract to open a second centre in a different part of Mumbai.

Amrita recalls this as a dark time for her personally. Bindu had always been at the heart of the running of the business and the division of roles worked beautifully. Bindu was expecting to be away for at least four years, and although she extended all the support she could from London, it was no substitute for her presence on the ground.

Bindu continued to support the business remotely from her home in England, using her time there to learn more about best practice in childcare. She enrolled her son into a daycare centre, even though she was at home, to get more direct exposure of how they functioned. She hoped that her the time spent researching and learning would help their business back in India.

Did Amrita feel like throwing in the towel at any point? She admits that she sometimes wondered if she could carry on after Bindu left. But what kept her going was the knowledge that there were people who depended on TLC for the care of their children and for their livelihood. The bond with Bindu and the relationship that Amrita had built up with the people who worked with her, who stayed with her to the end, were also sources of strength. "I can't understand people who say don't do business with friends. What kept TLC going was the deep friendship between Bindu and me."

At the time when Bindu was still in London, Amrita had come to realise that if the business was to grow sustainably, it needed to do so independently of their presence. She was convinced it had significant potential but she could not simultaneously manage the operations and focus on growth.

The combination of Bindu's move to London and their growth dilemma led them to consider taking on a third partner who had been recommended to them as a suitable candidate. The new partner, who was picked for his business development experience, was not previously known to either of them. His role was to help kick start the growth and expand their presence across the country beyond the four centres they had open at the time.

Not long after this addition was made to the team, in the aftermath of the financial crisis in the West, Bindu returned to India with her family and back into the TLC fold. Now there were three partners in the business and it was becoming apparent that their new partner had ambitions for the business that were at odds with Amrita's and Bindu's aspirations.

Exit from the business

Amrita and Bindu had grown their business entirely organically, i.e., without taking on debt finance or getting external investors in to help fuel growth. They realised that the business had reached "saturation point" and would need external funding to grow.

Bindu and Amrita are both firm believers in a personalised approach to business, but this became harder for them to maintain as the number of centres grew across different cities in India. They never seriously considered the idea of franchising their business for fear of losing that personal connection. They also enjoyed a strong loyalty from their employees, something they felt was not easy to replicate in a franchise model.

By 2013, they decided that it was time to find a buyer for the business, someone who would be able to finance faster growth. Amrita tells me the sale was not about the money or about finding the highest bidder. Having built the business from scratch, with a strong culture which put children first, they wanted to ensure that whoever bought it would carry on running the business as they had done. Amrita met the people who ran the business several times to ensure they had similar value systems to the ones they had at TLC.

They eventually sold TLC to their biggest competitor in India who operated on a slightly different model. It was the closest match to TLC in terms of culture. However, once it was sold Amrita and Bindu chose not to remain involved in the business.

Bindu aims to become a trainer in the specialist area of Mindfulness: a way of life that focuses on the present rather than the past. Amrita works with an organisation that does leadership coaching.

Lessons learnt and advice

- "Only do business with people you enjoy being with and spending time with – going to work should not be stressful."
- "Don't be afraid to grow your business on your own terms."
- "You must always strive to do better and evolve. Your clients and employees will respect you for that."
- "Treat all employees with respect."
- "Your personal warmth needs to come from within."
- "Be open-minded to receiving new information, that's how you learn and grow."
- "At the end of the day, what matters is how you execute your ideas."

"For two people to do business together, they either need to be on the same wavelength or complement each other. If those ingredients are missing, then managing personal conflicts and egos can take priority over managing the business."

CHAPTER 17

Emily Ellis
– Co-Founder, Flannel
Fingers – The UK

When Emily had an idea that would make her young children's bath times easier and safer, she and her husband Dave decided to turn it into a reality. Their vision is to supply all major retailers that stock mother and baby products.

Emily's A-ha! moment

The idea for Emily's business came to her during her daughters' bath time. As she struggled to both wash them and hold them secure because her hands were slippery with soap, Emily realised that the experience would be made so much easier if she had special gloves made with flannel cloth.

Emily searched in all the usual places to buy a pair but could find nothing that fitted the description. The idea stayed in her mind and a few months later she mentioned it to a couple of close friends who thought it was a clever business proposition. In June 2014, she and her husband Dave talked it over whilst on holiday and decided to bring Flannel Fingers to the market.

She recalls the time that her mother-in-law had handed her a magazine that fell open on an article about a mum who had started a business from home that was now in its fifth year. If she was looking for a sign, then this was it! Later she met this very same lady at a nursery fair she attended with her product samples. Meeting others who had similarly started with an idea and turned it into a business, gave Emily and Dave the courage and inspiration to go ahead with their idea.

Turning an idea into a business

What was it like for two people who had no business experience to get into setting one up from scratch? Emily admits they received some "conflicting advice" at first and they didn't really avail of any government help or take on a start-up loan. Instead, they checked the Internet for help and concluded that they needed the services of a design consultant that would help them with the design and manufacturing processes. It took nearly 18 months to get the design right, find the right suppliers for the raw material and to pick a suitable manufacturer. They also registered the design so that no one else was allowed to copy it.

At home, they converted one of the rooms into an office, paid a professional to create a website and social media presence, and got themselves on Amazon as a seller. Emily would go along to Nursery fairs and other Mother & Baby events to network and to market their new product. They have recently signed up a distributor to help them become a supplier to some well-known retailers of mother and baby products.

Product pricing and customer feedback

In order to determine the product's price, Emily checked the prices of similar products, such as bath mitts and exfoliating gloves. They decided early on that they needed to price them so they would be affordable to all mothers. They also foresaw a wider use of the flannel gloves in the care of elderly, the infirm or disabled. Having a self-imposed maximum price they could charge has helped them to stay disciplined in keeping costs down to a range that ensured the business could be profitable.

Customer feedback is very important to their business and creating a more disciplined way to collect and use feedback is on Emily's to-do list. It will also help them to direct their marketing efforts more effectively and improve their offering.

A partnership of equals

Their husband and wife team is a partnership based on complementary skills. Dave is better with the computer and IT-related issues, while Emily deals with the marketing side of the business. They both work on the financial side together. The business is young and there are plenty of ideas about how to grow it. They both continue to do their day jobs (Emily works part-time) and are taking things in small incremental steps. Emily's vision is to see her product on the shelves at UK retailers, such as Mothercare and Boots. Once these leaders start stocking her Finger Flannel gloves, the others may have no choice but to follow.

Lessons learnt and advice

- Sometimes you just have to learn on the job. "We now know so much more than we did when we first started out."
- Emily does not believe in looking back with regret. "Choose your path and be grateful for what comes along. Every time we feel a bit negative about something, something else comes along and makes it all worthwhile".

"How would you feel if you had a really good idea that you did nothing about only to find later that someone else turned it into a success? If you have an idea or a dream, just follow it."

CHAPTER 18

Jo Mondy
– Founder, Live Love Hoop
– The UK

When Jo set up Live Love Hoop, hula hooping was a novelty, even in the bohemian seaside town of Brighton. Thanks to her efforts and those of others, it is steadily becoming a more accepted way for adults and children to get fit in a fun and creative way.

Jo grew up in Sydney, Australia. In 2007, her best friend invited her along to a hula-hooping class. She found she wasn't particularly good at it at first, but once she got the hang of it, she found hooping both inspiring and addictive.

One day Jo's hoop teacher asked if she would cover her class in her absence and also perform in a group. She remembers being "terrified" at first. That was her first real experience of what was later to become her business. At this stage she was in a full-time job and hooping was just a hobby.

A fresh start and learning the ropes

In 2010, Jo moved to the UK with her then boyfriend. At first, she applied for jobs in the media and even got an offer that she declined because "it would have been the most boring job ever." Instead, setting up a hula-hooping business in their hometown of Brighton seemed like a perfect opportunity for a fresh start.

Jo taught herself to do all the business related things, such as registering the name of her business, creating flyers for marketing purposes and getting to grips with her finances. She got help and advice from peers and fellow hula-hoopers around the world. One of her students, who happened to be an accountant, helped her enormously in the early days.

Being new to the town (and the country) Jo had very few friends of her own in the area. So she did her early networking within her then boyfriend's social circles. Once she had picked a venue for her classes, she put the word out and posted her flyers all around town. She also joined Circus Spinning sessions that helped her to make further connections.

Establishing a new market

Back then hula hooping was a relatively unknown leisure and fitness activity even in Brighton, which today teems with spinning hula-hoops. Finding the right format and pricing formula for her classes involved some research and a lot of trial and error. She checked pricing on classes for similar disciplines and used that as a guide.

At first, she tried "drop-in" classes where people did not book in advance and just dropped in on the day. She found this didn't work, mainly because the outcome was completely unpredictable. Some days no one would turn up and other days there would be too many to fit in the hall. The high cost of hiring venues in Brighton also made it a challenge. She instead opted for a structure where people signed up for a beginners' course, which included a series of classes paid for by students in advance, and created a natural demand for her handmade hula-hoops.

What was it like in the early days to teach a diverse group of people with different abilities and attitudes to learning? "As I've become more experienced I can gauge what the student's emotional state is and will go off-piste if necessary." Jo doesn't think she has ever had a "difficult" student. In her experience, students who struggle are often the least confident. Jo always got feedback after every course and had personal conversations with students to understand what worked and what needed to be finessed.

She tells me about a time when a man and his 11-year-old-son came to one of her beginners' courses. It was unusual to have men in her classes, even though there are some amazing male hoopers out there. It was their father-son activity and they diligently came every week. The boy, Aidan, was very shy at first but progressed well and got really good. She tells me he signed up to the Hooping Idol competition organised by Hooping.org, where he made excellent progress even if he did not go on to win.

Effective marketing through networking

In the early days, Jo found she did "a lot of stuff for free". This was partly motivated by her desire to create awareness of her business and also to make new friends who enjoyed the same things as she did. She was building a solid base of hula-hoopers in Brighton. By providing free events where they could learn from each other and improve, she was helping to create a community of hoopers. Furthermore, the colourful hoops spinning away in the summer sunshine became a most excellent promotional tool, attracting tourists to her classes.

Aside from word of mouth and the flyers she used, what other marketing tools does she use? "Events and Social Media are a really important way of communicating." In the beginning, she did most things herself, including creating her website. She is self-deprecating about her early attempts at the online aspects of her business for which she now has a bit more professional help. Her husband Andy is more of an expert on all things digital and helps her in an unofficial capacity.

Early lessons

When Jo first started out she was teaching every night of the week and was also doing a "boot camp" to enhance her own fitness. A couple of years of this and she was physically exhausted and felt "completely wiped out". It was a scary time for Jo and made her realise that her punishing schedule was allowing her no time to unwind. She now teaches more condensed classes over fewer days a week. This ensures that she gets full days off each week.

Jo also recalls losing money in the early days because she agreed to gigs without fully understanding or mutually agreeing the terms and conditions. The lessons she learnt was to get everything down in writing, so there could be no ambiguity should things not go as planned.

She warns that it is tempting to view being busy all the time as a sign of success. "If you feel you are not enjoying the classes then it is a warning sign", that you may be overworked and burning out. She has learnt not to put undue pressure on herself if she finds that she is not feeling up to it.

When your hobby turns into a business, how do you keep it fresh? "Finding time to refresh and learn is hard when you are a full-time hula-hooper," admits Jo. She teaches an advanced class who are very good and her students give her the motivation to learn more. She also attends hoop conventions and gatherings where she can share ideas and inspiration with fellow hoopers.

Spotting an adjacent niche

Jo confesses that she was surprised at the success of her business. She had given it a year at the outset to see if it was viable. As the hooping community continued to grow and thrive in her local area, she spotted a gap in the market. There was no one in the UK who was doing hoop teacher training, which gave would-be hoop teachers the tools to teach in their own unique style, as most established teaching programmes were franchise models that allowed for very little personal creativity. She had informally been doing this already, as she had trained up a few people to cover her classes when she was unable to do them.

Jo found that this idea proved very popular. She did three weekend sessions in her first year that were all fully subscribed. Not only were hoopers from all over the country coming down for her courses, her popularity had spread to Europe. She was recently asked to conduct courses in Slovenia and Austria. She is able to do this without it taking too much extra effort in putting the course material together because "a lot of the material is not site specific: the goal setting for instance". She expects to do more of these, but only on demand.

Jo continues to rely on word of mouth for most of her marketing. She is in the process of revamping her website and looking to add new features. She is also planning the next level of teacher's training in due course. Teaching online is also an option. She has been reluctant to go down that route in the past because others are already doing it, but now she has the confidence to go ahead and will try to use technology more extensively in her business.

Medium to long-term vision

What is Jo's vision for Live Love Hoop in five years' time? Over the coming years, she hopes to create a business that will not solely rely on her. She wants to use her brand to create opportunities that will allow her to step back and let others do it for her. She wants to do more self-contained events, such as hen parties, as well as more online lessons. She would also like to be part of the government's programme to encourage young people to get more active and hopes to work closely with her local council and schools. "Live Love Hoop started off as something that was part time, but I want to now make it into a more sustainable business," says Jo.

Lessons learnt and advice

- "Make sure your passion stays your passion. Make sure you don't lose the joy in it. Always remember the reason why you share what you want to share."
- "Make sure you create downtime. You need a day a week to switch off."
- "Make sure you cover your costs. That is essential if you are ever to build a viable business."

"Build a network and community of people who are in a similar headspace as you. Friends and family are great, but you want someone whom you can bounce ideas off and get a rational response to a problem."

CHAPTER 19

Leila Dewji
– Co-Founder, I_AM SELF
PUBLISHING – The UK

Leila's self-publishing business offers lesser-known and brand new authors the chance to have their work published, easy access to the e-reader market and greater control over the royalties from their book.

Leila started her career in trade publishing and she then became a literary agent. Her role was to nurture and develop an author's talent before pitching their manuscript to big publishing houses.

Leila's A-ha! moment

Back in the day, publishers viewed their business as a numbers game. Not all their authors would be successful, but those that were would more than make up for the cost of those that were less successful. When the financial crisis hit in 2008, the publishing houses were hit hard and didn't take on many new authors. Most publishers became extremely risk averse and were only interested in well-known authors. This was frustrating for Leila. After all the time she had spent nurturing new authors, there was nowhere for them to go with all the publishers saying 'no'.

This gave Leila the idea to set up her own self-publishing business. Her research had shown her that the prevailing self-publishing business model at the time was an extension of the printing business, without sufficient attention to detail. This was also the time when e-books were becoming popular in the US and demand for Kindles in the UK was just starting to pick up. Leila believed there was huge potential for digital publishing.

Finding a business partner

Leila spent about a year researching and thinking about her new business idea. At the time her brother Ali was working in magazine publishing, an industry that had been already forced to transition from paper to digital. His strengths were in marketing and public relations, whereas Leila had the contacts, as she had built up personal working relationships with both established and budding authors. Their complementary skills made the decision to go into business together a relatively easy one.

In 2010, Leila and Ali set up I_AM SELF-PUBLISHING. The initial focus was on e-book creations for established authors who already had an established print readership. By going digital, via a self-publishing route, these authors now had a way to cut out the middlemen who often took 90 per cent of their royalties. By going digital via the self-publishing route, it was possible for the author to retain the vast majority of the royalties.

Whom did Leila and Ali turn to for help when setting up their new business? "At that time Business Link, a government-funded organisation, was a useful reference point. I also read *How To Start A Business – Dummies Guide*. And when we set up our business bank account the bank was very helpful, providing us with templates and a helpline," remembers Leila.

They realised there was a lot of interest and potential demand for their services in the first year, but you have to "put yourself out there" via networking events, such as trade fairs. Thanks to Leila's contacts from her previous work experience, there were a few authors on their books even before they had started the business, giving them the confidence to go ahead.

Establishing credibility in the market

Before formally launching their business, they did a few free jobs for people to ensure the system and the printing worked. There was a lot of word of mouth, and before long other agencies started referring authors to them. Early marketing initiatives included a writing competition with the winner getting a free e-book published.

They created a website by first drawing out how they wanted it to look. Leila and Ali did a lot of the basic stuff themselves and only got a developer to help finesse it in the latter stages. They chose to keep the layout clean and uncluttered. "A number of the competitors have an EasyJet model: the cost escalates as you keep adding a bewildering number of options to your basket. We wanted to give our customers clarity in terms of what can get from us," says Leila.

Giving customers value for money

At first, their pricing strategy was to undercut the competition as a way to win business. She admits that in the early days they underestimated the operational costs. With time and experience, they have learnt to recognise which aspects of their service were non-essential to the overall outcome and changed the offer. This reduces their cost and consequently the price the customer pays.

When we talk about customer satisfaction and the feedback mechanism, Leila explains that feedback is typically results driven, in terms of how well the book has done relative to the author's own expectations. Happy customers tend to recommend their services to other authors. If a client is unhappy it is usually because they have misunderstood what they are getting into and what they can expect in return for the price quoted.

Over time, both Leila and Ali have become more adept at recognising who is likely to be a difficult customer. When they were younger and just starting out, they didn't want to turn any business away. They also found they were doing "lots of extras" just to keep the client happy. Experience has taught them to "trust their gut instinct" when taking on a new client. They have got better at managing expectations, so the client knows exactly what is being offered to them before they go ahead.

Is there a danger of their business being disrupted by even more DIY versions of self-publishing, where the authors can do everything for themselves by using online platforms? "Authors want someone who cares about their work," she says. "Big publishers don't provide a personal service. Authors want to feel reassured that their baby is in good hands." She also points out that there are many aspects of self-publishing, for instance proof reading, the design of the book cover and the marketing of the book, that the author may not be equipped to handle by themselves. Seeking professional guidance can increase the chances of a successful book launch.

Funding the business

How did they finance the business in the early days? Leila admits they were fortunate because both she and Ali had moved back to living with their mother, and so were not under much financial pressure. Besides, the initial costs were low since it is a service-based business and they self-financed them. Leila admits, "There was a fair amount of trial and error though, and we had to educate ourselves along the way."

About a year and a half into the running of the business, they felt comfortable enough to move into an office. "Working from home was not ideal," Leila says, as she found it hard to draw the line between her work and downtime, especially in the early days when "the to-do list was endless".

"When we first started we were very young and made mistakes. Even though Ali had studied business management, running your own business is very different."

Being self-financed has allowed Leila and Ali to remain in control of their business, be dynamic and change things if they didn't work. However, looking back now, Leila and Ali wonder if it might have been better at some point to seek funding to help them grow faster and scale up.

Collaborating with other professionals

Like many young businesses, they rely on freelancers who get paid for specific projects. Even people who have 9 to 5 jobs are often on the lookout for side projects. They took on someone on a part-time basis to help with admin once they had moved into an office. Taking on employees is a big decision when you are the owner of a start-up because "you find you are paying someone else more per hour than you are yourself".

Working with a sibling with complementary skills has been a good formula and they have both learnt so much through having to become "Jack of all trades." "We didn't know much about digital marketing. We had to pick up new skills," says Leila.

They also sought external help on things that were not in their zone of expertise. "The online content for the website and our social media presence is done in-house. But we work with a search engine optimisation (SEO) expert who helps us with our search rankings."

Lessons learnt and advice

- "Do your research and be really sure of the gap in the market you are seeking to fill."
- "Don't copy what's already there. Find something unique that solves a problem."
- "Spend the larger part of your research on determining whom you will be selling to."

"The biggest part of the business plan is the marketing. You need to understand your target demographic and be consistent with your messaging from day one."

CHAPTER 20

Raga Olga D'Silva – Co-Founder, Speaking Minds – The UK

It was an epiphany in the boardroom that led Raga into entrepreneurship. Speaking Minds, previously known as RHM Global, creates platforms for building personal brands and hosting corporate events worldwide.

Raga had a highly successful career in Advertising and Marketing that began in 1990 in India. Her last senior role there was as Vice-President and Branch Head for Lintas Direct Mumbai in 2000. A year later she moved to New Zealand with her family and re-started her career. Within a short time, Raga had risen to a senior level within the advertising industry and joined the top one per cent of earners in the country. But she gave it up in order to set up her venture to support international companies from the around the world to do business in India. As part of this, she was invited on to the board of the India New Zealand Business Council (INZBC) and became the first woman to hold the position. She recounts how she was sitting in a boardroom surrounded by "suits" when she just knew she "could not do this anymore." She felt a strong urge to become an entrepreneur and no additional incentives from her employer could persuade her to stay.

Entrepreneurship beckons

She realised it was time for her to do something with India and use her acumen, networks, knowledge and experience to her advantage and that's how Global Village Unlimited, the first incarnation of her current business, was born in 2007. At that time India was one of the shining lights in the emerging world and all businesses wanted to be part of the country's growth. Interestingly, on the same evening that she had resigned, Raga had a call from someone who wanted her help to get better acquainted with India with a view to doing business there.

"When you put out something to the universe, it just always comes back to you," she says, remembering that serendipitous phone call. Raga had a "fantastic network" of people whom she had previously done business with in India and was now able to tap into. "All I had to do was create some strategic thoughts and a business model. When you do good work, your network will always stand up for you. Nothing is more important than delivering on your promise".

The original business model was based on the idea of connecting people outside of India with business and marketing opportunities within the country. At first, it centred around helping businesses and individuals to successfully navigate their way in a new country with all its complexities. But it grew into a knowledge business that designed premium seminars and workshops to corporate clients by using some highly influential people from around the world. For instance, she hosted Edward de Bono, the guru of lateral thinking, getting him access to the Indian corporate world. She also organised seminars for Deepak Chopra and Stephen Covey, amongst others in various countries, including NZ, Australia, China, Hong Kong, Singapore and India.

Turning crisis into opportunity

Things were going well until the global financial crisis hit, followed by a recession at the end of 2008. As a result, corporate clients no longer had the budget to invest in these kinds of events. Overnight, her income plummeted and she recalls the dark time when she had "lost everything and did not even have enough money to buy a slice of bread for my children".

During that time she did a number of consulting jobs on the side to generate an income whilst she considered ways to make her business more resilient. "Being a boutique business is hard but you need absolute belief in yourself that no matter what, you have it in you to provide for your family." Raga decided the business model had to change; it needed to be more immune to the vicissitudes of the economy and the business cycle of her clients.

She had discovered that there were a number of high achievers and public speakers around the world that were simply not getting enough work, or if they were, they were not able to adequately commercialise their skills. For instance, Mark Inglis, a renowned double amputee whose remarkable feat of climbing Mount Everest had earned him many speaking engagements, approached her. These events had not, however, been monetised fully and Raga realised she could help. She had spotted a gap in the market for individuals who are role models or influential in their own field of specialisation to get help in creating their own personal brand.

Finding a business partner

It was around this time that Raga met Nicola Fenton, who later went on to become Raga's business partner. She was Senior Business Head with the global catering giant Compass Group, managing the hospitality and facilities at the New Zealand Parliament. Nicola had also previously spent time in the UK as part of the team that set up the hospitality at Tate Modern in London. Her experience and expertise were highly relevant, and she had many of the skills that Raga knew she was lacking.

"I was very clear about what my strengths and weaknesses were. I needed someone to take care of the areas where I knew I was weak, such as managing money (I was good at making money, just not managing it), managing resources and logistics. Nicola had the experience of these things and so we found a beautiful synergy." Raga's view is that it did not matter that the two had not known each other previously because what mattered was that they complemented each other so well.

Was it difficult going from being the sole owner to having an equal partner joining the business? "I hang out with different entrepreneurs and some prefer to remain a one-person show. I have always wanted to leave a legacy. I'm not precious about anything in life (other than my children) and so it was always a plan to scale it up one day. And that means bringing in new people into the business who bring more than just money."

Building a new business identity

In early 2010, both Raga and Nicola were in India with a view to incorporating their business there. Raga tells the story of how Global Village Unlimited got renamed as Red Hot Mirchi (RHM). They had to send a broad selection of possible names for the Indian officials to pick, so as to minimise the risk of having them all rejected. They had made a list of about ten potential names, including the prevailing name Global Village Unlimited. Most were variations on that name and conveyed the same meaning. But by the time they had reached the tenth name they had run out of ideas. Raga looked around the kitchen for inspiration when she spotted some red chillies that her mother had set aside as she cooked. As luck would have it, Red Hot Mirchi was the name chosen by the officials. Raga admits that she disliked the name at first, but she later realised that it made them stand out and proved to be a great icebreaker with people she had never met before.

After registering the business in India, they set up an office in New Delhi to help them with the back office function and in 2014, set up a call centre and a marketing office in Durgapur, a town about 200km from Kolkata, that employed only women. "I've always been willing to experiment," says Raga. Durgapur has steel mills and other heavy industry that attracts educated young men, mostly engineers from Kolkata. But the wives of these men have no opportunities in the small town. RHM was able to tap into this community, creating a win-win for all concerned.

The evolution of the business model

How did they go about reinventing their business and winning customers? "Our customers are the corporate clients we organise speaking events for. We also design the framework for client and employee engagement needs, including conferences and team building offsite events. But our speakers are also our customers. It is our job to keep both sides happy because if we don't deliver on the promise we will not get further business". It is this attention to detail that has earned RHM the respect of an enviable list of inspirational speakers, performers, thought leaders and trainers who are on their books, which has, in turn, attracted a blue chip customer base of corporate clients. But she has found that managing the egos and the conflicting demands of the two sides can be a challenge.

"The way you manage people when you are young is different to when you are older. When I was 28, I was the youngest leader for Lintas and was managing a large and very experienced team. I had people who were older than me in my team. The way I dealt with conflict then was very different; I may have burnt a lot of bridges. I wouldn't do that now."

How does she find the balance and can she share any anecdotes about these challenging situations? She gives me the example of a live situation for an upcoming event, where her client is a corporation that only ever works with the highest quality people and is very demanding. The speaker, on the other hand, is also a "big guy himself and runs a multi-billion dollar corporation". He is highly experienced at public speaking with his own way of doing things. The corporate client has laid out some very specific needs in terms of how they want the speaker to present, whilst the speaker is adamant about doing the talk his own way. "We will just have to find a way to get both sides to agree before the actual event," Raga says, in the tone of someone who has seen this many times before.

Raga recounts another incident that has stayed in her mind. They had just got going with their new business model in 2009/10 and had an event in New Delhi organised for a well-known public speaker. Based in the US, this highly acclaimed thought leader and author in the area of health and wellness was accustomed to selling out venues. But the Indian economy was still in the doldrums and they had barely sold 500 tickets in a 2,000-seater auditorium. She contacted the speaker to ask if they should cancel the event but he didn't want to. Raga shudders as she remembers how they had to fill the auditorium by giving tickets away and enticing people to come along, a ploy that resulted in a calibre of audience that was not quite what it could have been. Not only was the event a financial disaster but they also had a very unhappy client. If a situation like that occurred today, she is clear she would act differently. "I would go with my gut instinct and cancel the event, which is what I had wanted to do that time too."

Competition

Who does Raga view as her competitors and how is her business different? "We have a lot of competition, including businesses that operate from home. They may have one or two celebrity speakers for whom they act as agents." She explains that these types of agencies are referred to as Speakers Bureau. Some might have exclusive rights to all the Speaker's engagements and would typically earn a percentage of whatever the Speaker gets paid. "Our main business is knowledge driven for which there are not many competitors." RHM is not just a Speakers Bureau, it builds brands and creates the right image for each speaker, making them more marketable and extending their reach to a wider audience. It also offers many services that are completely unique to RHM Global.

Work-life balance: shunning limiting belief systems

Raga's work is clearly very demanding and requires her to travel extensively for days on end. How does she find a work-life balance? Raga tells me firmly that she doesn't think about life in that way. "Balance is not just about family and professional life. Women have hundreds of boxes (to tick) and we have to find a way to manage them all. People often feel unfulfilled because they feel they can't do it all. I don't believe in limiting belief systems. I have moved with my children and lived in three different countries. Even when my children were really young and I had to travel on business for 19 days, I packed their clothes individually for each day and made a detailed spreadsheet of everything that needed to be done for them and gave this to the people who would be taking care of them in my absence. My kids have turned out alright; they are 18 now."

Raga claims that she has never let her responsibilities be a limiting factor and neither should anyone else. She has also never had a ready-made support system, but instead built one up herself, every step of the way. "There should be no reason not to follow your heart, be it in life or in business."

Raga's long-term vision

What is Raga's definition of success? "It is a highly personal thing and means different things to different people," she says. RHM has reached its goal three years sooner than they had planned and they are now getting ready for the next step in its growth phase. She is about to travel to India where she is hoping to conclude a deal which will see RHM joining hands with another entity that has deeper pockets and the strategic vision the business needs in order to scale up.

At the time of publication of the book, her business has been renamed Speaking Minds and added two new partners: Milind Soman, India's first male supermodel, actor, and promoter of fitness for women through India's biggest women's running event, the Pinkathon; and Reema Sanghvi, Founder of Maximus MICE, a company that specialises in premium events for corporates. With these new business partners on board Raga believes their service offering is stronger and more extensive than before.

Lessons learnt and advice

- "You have to absolutely believe in what you are doing and treat it as a commitment to yourself."
- "Don't be afraid to take that first step, stop looking for the right time. Do it now!"
- "Don't do it for the money. Money should not be the driving force for starting a business. If money is the main object, then stay in a salaried job."
- "Don't limit yourself. Find a reason to make it happen, don't look for excuses to not make it happen."
- "Always, always deliver on your promise. Don't overpromise."
- "Don't forget to give back."

"Set yourself a big target, but break it into smaller goals. But once you reach your goal, push it further and set more challenging ones. Every time you achieve a goal, remember to celebrate success."

CHAPTER 21

Raka Chakrawarti – Founder, GourmetDelight – India

Raka's long experience within the Taj Group of Hotels prepared her well for entrepreneurship. GourmetDelight is an online delicatessen where customers can buy high-quality prepared foods and hard-to-find food ingredients.

Raka spent many years working for the Taj Group of Hotels in India, most recently in Public Relations. The Food and the Restaurant aspect of the business held particular interest for her and she has huge respect for the chefs who work under enormous pressure in commercial kitchens.

The business idea

Raka had observed that a number of hotel restaurant customers were interested in the recipes of the dishes they ate and wanted to know more about the ingredients that went into them. This observation, combined with the knowledge that a number of these ingredients were not easily available in the desired quality, got her thinking about the opportunity to connect quality suppliers with buyers. This was the origin of Gourmet Delight.

She had been mulling over the idea for two years and had used the time to research the opportunity. Since then she has signed up over 200 suppliers, both locally and from outside India, who now find a platform for their produce via gourmetdelight.in – an online portal for organic produce and high-quality food ingredients.

Establishing the business opportunity

Raka conducted some initial research to ensure there was a viable business opportunity with sufficient customer demand. In the early days, she visited stores that might supply similar ingredients to check prices and quality, and talked to customers to find out what prices they were willing to pay for organic produce.

The market for organic food in India is fairly nascent and mostly linked with mothers of younger children, the elderly and health conscious people. However, there is a growing awareness of its merits, especially in a city like Mumbai, where Raka says, "Once people start buying organic they are likely to remain hooked."

GourmetDelight does not have any stores and currently its website is its only storefront. Launched in April 2015, its early version was a "Beta platform that was very basic" but helped them to get initial feedback and learn from their mistakes. In December 2015, they moved to an improved website which is currently in use.

In the early days, Raka recalls that they could not correctly estimate distances to the customers' address, which had an impact on delivery times. There were also occasional delays in receiving goods from suppliers. This created problems, as it would have a knock-on impact on their ability to fulfil customer orders. At other times, there were mistakes in packaging and some customers even received the wrong product. "But we corrected each mistake immediately, quite unlike what happens in the corporate world" where mistakes are often missed or overlooked.

Customer engagement and word of mouth

Raka estimates that 70-80 per cent of her business comes from people who visit the website. "Once customers start buying, they are likely to recommend the name to friends and family. Word of mouth works for us, we are not really spending on advertising."

Does she gather customer feedback and how does it influence the way the business operates? Having worked for an organisation that goes to great lengths to win over an unhappy customer, Raka understands well the importance of customer satisfaction. In the early days, if a customer were unhappy with the product they received, she would offer a no quibbles replacement. "A complaining customer is always treated with respect. We always try to help [resolve the situation]." But as the business grew, it became economically unviable to immediately replace goods, especially without charging for delivery. Now she offers customers alternatives that incentivise the customer to come back and re-order.

Getting regular feedback from customers is a core part of the operating strategy. "We have a process of calling customers over the phone to get feedback, especially customers who have drifted off and haven't come back." By calling them on the telephone, she ensures there is a personal connection and a dialogue that can result in a richer interaction than by simply bombarding them with emails or texts.

Building the business infrastructure

How did Raka deal with all the rules, regulations and licencing requirements that trading in food products entails? Raka admits that experience of working in the hotel industry's property division prepared her for what was needed in terms of licencing requirements and food safety rules. This has enabled her to expand the offering on her website to include "artisan products" prepared by home chefs. She hand picks the chefs who prepare these dishes in their own homes, but only once they have been thoroughly vetted and licensed for food safety.

In terms of the infrastructure and logistics, she hires people who take delivery of perishable produce that mainly comes from Pune, a few hours drive away, and then start packing it for delivery to customers. She has an equal number of men and women working for her, but finds the women tend to be "more organised, dedicated to what they do, love the product and are more likely to point out things that are intuitive to them. The men just want to get things done and currently do most of the deliveries."

Raka hopes that the women will get more involved in delivering the food in future, so that they will have more direct customer engagement and be able to deal with unhappy customers more effectively. This makes sense since her customers are also more likely to be women.

A career that prepared Raka for entrepreneurship

Raka admits that the ten years she spent at the Taj Group of Hotels prepared her well for this entrepreneurial venture, as the organisation gives its employees exposure to different aspects of its business. However, she admits that her teenage daughter's generation may not feel the need to take that route. "If you are young and have an idea, then time is on your side."

Raka is supported by her husband Himanshu, who is himself a successful businessman and co-founder of her business. She also has a "wonderful network of chefs" who keep her informed on what's trending, as well as what's new and yet to become mainstream. Some of these chefs also provide her with artisan products, like cakes she can retail via her website.

What is it like to be her own boss and be responsible for the livelihood of others? "In my old job, I was very careful about my me-time. Now I have less time for myself but I am no longer tied to someone else's expectations. I don't feel the stress because I love it and feel this was meant to be for me." Raka is also keen to support small suppliers. "Their passion is what drives me," she explains.

Raka's vision for her business

"We are currently looking at potential partners [who will provide funding], but want somebody who really understands the specialised niche we are in; someone who can also bring in expertise or technology [to enable more efficient order fulfilment]." Raka is clear that despite her ambitions to grow and expand into other major cities in India, she has no intention of turning it into a mass-market proposition.

Raka aims to be involved in the business for as long as she can and she has the full support of her family in this. She would like to see GourmetDelight listed on the Indian stock market some day. She firmly believes the time is right for a business like hers, given that people are becoming more aware of what they eat.

Lessons learnt and advice

"Before you jump in to become an entrepreneur you have to ask yourself the following questions:

- Do you really want to do it?
- Do you understand it well enough: the legal, the commercial, operational, technology and logistics issues?
- You may not possess all the skills. Unlike in a corporate environment where there are people doing different roles, in your own business you have to do everything until you can find, and afford, the right people to do them for you.
- You should be prepared to firefight every day and face the challenges. Would you be willing to sweat it out?"

"Don't leave a corporate career to dive into entrepreneurship as a more relaxed option, where you work for yourself. You need to have extra reserves of strength and money. You may have to give up holidays, friends and other interests. Are you prepared to stick it out?"

CHAPTER 22

Sangita Joshi – Co-Founder, EmPower Research – India

It has been five years since Sangita and her three co-founders sold EmPower Research to a bigger US-based competitor. She offers a case study on how it is possible to identify a gap in the market and turn it into a successful business with limited upfront investment.

Sangita is a Mechanical Engineer by qualification who went on to complete a post-graduate programme in management at IIM Bangalore. She had a successful corporate career working at multinationals, including Gillette and Whirlpool. She has also taught at several business schools and is a freelance writer for business newspapers in India.

How it all began

The credit for spotting the business opportunity goes to Debjani Deb who was at the time working for the PR firm GCI in the USA and went on to start up EmPower Research. Debjani had observed that PR agencies tended to focus more on the creative aspect of their service and did not have the time, the resources or the skill to really understand the business their client was in. She saw an opportunity to close this gap by creating an entity that would specialise in providing timely business research to PR firms, who could then create a more coherent and relevant public relations strategy on behalf of their clients.

Debjani mentioned this idea to her boss at GCI, and with his blessings decided to set up an offshore entity based in India. The second member to join the team was Debjani's cousin, Shoma Bakre. At the time, Shoma was looking to move back to India from the US, along with her family and was happy to help set up the business in India. They next decided to find someone with relevant work experience in India to work with Shoma and started the search for the third founding member, which culminated in Sangita also becoming a co-founder. The fourth and last member of the founding team was Kyung Han, a former colleague of Debjani who lived in New York and took on the role of client services in the US.

At the time that Sangita was first approached, she had quit active corporate life after the birth of her daughter and was teaching in business schools on a freelance basis. Sangita met Shoma and Debjani over a coffee and agreed to help out by doing web-based research for them from the comfort of her own home. "It was all very informal," recalls Sangita. "I was distracted because I had left my baby with a babysitter and we just swapped telephone numbers on paper napkins."

Arbitraging freely available information

They realised that there was so much information freely available on the web that someone with business sense and experience could package it up in a way that is far less expensive than doing primary research or hiring a consultant. In Sangita's words, "it was quick and dirty and gave options to clients in terms of how they could respond to a particular situation".

It was the summer of 2004. Debjani's former employer GCI gave them a test project to work on. Sangita remembers producing a deck of information that laid out the roadmap from a business and a public relations angle with possible courses of action. "The team at GCI loved it so much they gave it a standing ovation," chuckles Sangita. They had provided the client with a very good brief for creating a PR campaign and this was when EmPower really became a business and GCI formalised the relationship by becoming their first client.

Target market

In terms of potential customers, they focused on the PR industry. The PR firms lapped up the service as it made life easier for them, helping them provide a more timely response to their clients. Debjani tapped into an excellent network of contacts within the PR and Advertising world and would "pound the streets", looking to drum up business. The work was then sent back to Sangita and Shoma in India, invariably on a Friday, which meant they found themselves working over weekends to produce reports for clients in time for Monday morning in the USA.

Pricing strategy and growing on a shoestring budget

In the early days, when EmPower was finding its feet, they kept their prices deliberately low. Once clients could see the value in their work, it was easier to upsell them more services at a higher price. It offered a very good value proposition to new clients.

Within four to five months they found they were getting so much work that they needed help to complete it. None of them had ever run a company before and for as long as possible shared the workload amongst themselves. But as the orders starting rolling in, Sangita and Shoma "roped in friends and family, and those who had time and wanted to do some useful work." It suited them well. "It was a flexible way of tapping into a network of 25-30 people, mostly women," says Sangita. These ladies had given up corporate careers for personal reasons but were keen to remain productive. "The domain was so broad, we needed more specialisation in areas such as technology, marketing, etc. We needed to train them and ensure they conformed with the deck we were using to win clients." The network operated really well and the team had successfully put in place processes for supervision.

There came a point when they realised they could no longer just operate from their respective homes and decided it was time to set up an office in India. Suddenly they had to navigate rules and regulations, and the bureaucracy that was new to them. Fortunately, they found someone at a Chartered Accountancy firm who would take care of all the administration, accountancy and human resources functions for them. In terms of office space, at first they hired an office in a business centre on a pay per use basis.

It was just a 6'x8' cubicle inside a sophisticated business centre. Sangita recalls a time when a client was visiting from the US and wanted to see their offices. They gave him a tour of the impressive business centre and let him believe that the whole building was theirs!

"We bootstrapped very efficiently until we were very certain of recurring revenues. We never bit off more than we could chew", especially when it came to incurring fixed costs. In addition, EmPower's revenues were in US Dollars but most of their costs were in Rupees. With the dollar remaining strong for most of the time, this favoured their business. Initially, they were doing a lot of work that earned them $5,000 - $10,000 per contract: useful bread and butter business, but still not enough to give them the certainty they needed to really invest in the next stage of growth.

Growing up and finding an adjacent growth opportunity

Winning their "first proper consulting project, requiring both primary and secondary research" was a significant milestone. They earned $140,000 for it and the project gave them the confidence to make their first senior hire: a lady who took on responsibility for the team's research output.

Social media was now taking hold, which offered them an opportunity to figure out what people were thinking before it became mainstream news. They were in the right place at the right time, but serendipity favours those who are both well prepared and brave. EmPower soon jumped from being a company that mainly provided tailored secondary research services into a digital media and analytics company.

The team tapped into the team's rapidly growing young IT talent to "develop a methodology and technology that could harness public opinion to influence business strategy." This led to winning a contract to do media monitoring for a PR company. This proved to be a vital tool for corporate clients, especially in cases of crisis communication, self-inflicted or otherwise. The time difference between the US and India was a real bonus. It allowed the team in India to carry out research while it was night in the US, and then deliver a report to the client by early morning US time. This meant the PR firm was typically armed with information and proposals before their client needed to make any public announcements to the stock market. In the absence of this help, it was not uncommon for PR executives to start their working day at 3am.

Unsurprisingly, the PR firms and their clients valued this service, particularly in industries such as the pharmaceutical industry where the confidence of customers and the regulators is critical to the success of their business. The media monitoring service enabled clients to be proactive, rather than reactive, and pick any changes in perception or trends early on. PR firms had also found the EmPower's services useful when themselves pitching for new business.

A low upfront cost business model

The business was cash flow positive from day one. The advantage of being a service industry is that there are very low fixed costs at the outset. The co-founders did not take a salary from the business for the first four years, choosing instead to put profits back into growing the business. This meant that EmPower's growth was self-funded, allowing the founders to remain in full control.

"We had a no-frills approach to costs. We focused on hiring fresh graduates who were cheaper but had to be trained and developed." All non-core functions, such as HR and Accounts, were outsourced at first. They were very fortunate to have an excellent firm of Chartered Accountants who provided them with all these services until they were ready to create a permanent role within the firm.

Being a primarily female-led organisation in a male chauvinistic society had its pitfalls. Sangita recalls being treated like "second-class citizens" by their landlord they had leased office space from. Sangita and Shoma were made to "wait outside" his office for ages, and he then tried to "fleece" them by changing the terms of their agreed deal. Sangita recalls how a partner from their chartered accountant firm came along "like a knight in shining armour" and sorted things out for them.

Effective team building

The same gentleman who gallantly rode to their rescue, later with the blessings of his employer joined EmPower as a permanent member of their senior team, in charge of their financial accounts. They also hired a senior person with business processing experience who was given responsibility for their administrative function, while the senior hire of a woman to head up the HR function was deemed as "transformational".

Sangita admits they were lucky to have found people who were not only excellent but also stayed with the firm right to the end. A well-run human resources department lies at the heart of any business that relies on the quality and productivity of the people who work for it.

The dynamic between the four founders

What was the working relationship between the four co-founders and how did they deal with differences of opinion? The question is particularly relevant, as they had been serendipitously thrown together with no prior personal connection in most cases. "We were four very different people but with complementary skill sets. In the beginning, we were all over each other and talked daily over the telephone. The ongoing communication was critical. At first, everyone tried to do everything, but over time developed individual roles that each was best suited for." She jokingly describes them as "hunter, farmer, producer and processor". She took care of the "factory end" with Shoma, whilst the two partners in the US were responsible for finding new clients and servicing them.

There were personality clashes but these were always resolved, as they all knew they had a shared purpose and needed to find a way to work together. They would help each other, which included giving and listening to feedback.

Vision for the business: an exit plan

As EmPower went from strength to strength, it attracted the interest of firms who wanted to either acquire it or take a stake in the business. But the firm did not need funding and as the dynamic between the four founders was good, they did not want to risk adding a new partner.

Did the founders ever discuss an exit plan? About seven years had passed since they had first started the business and the female founders, in particular, felt burnt out. They had young children and "felt the need to take a breather". An Indian firm made an offer for the business at around this time but the founders did not think the price was attractive enough and decided to open up the bidding process to attract wider interest from firms based in India and abroad.

In September 2011, Genpact, a global leader in the management of business processes and technology, acquired

EmPower. At the time, EmPower had 360 employees, based in New York, Bangalore, Cincinnati, New Jersey, San Francisco, and London.

Lessons learnt and advice

Sangita's advice is particularly aimed at anyone looking to go into a technology-based or service-based business.

- "The service sector is easy to get started and if run well, is very soon cash positive. But it is harder to scale up."
- "These days, start-ups tend to need technology products. There is a danger of moving too far away from the core proposition by customising the product too much."

"The vision should be evolutionary and every client's requirement will need to feed into the core of your product. This will affect everything: the way you run your business, how you live and how you price your product/service."

CHAPTER 23

Sharda Agarwal – Co-Founder, Sepalika – India

Sharda and her co-founder Mahesh Jayaraman are on a very personal quest to help people make informed choices about their own health. The website is in its first year and their focus is on driving high-quality and relevant content so it becomes the "go-to" site for information on dietary supplements.

After completing a post graduate programme in management from IIM Bangalore, Sharda spent 22 years in branding and marketing, including jobs at the global giants Johnson & Johnson and Coca-Cola. She and a former colleague then set up a consultancy that provided advice to multinationals on strategy and branding matters.

There came a time when she was no longer "enthused" by what she was doing because, in essence, the "nature of the work had been the same" for too long. The consultancy was successful and during the ten-year period she was part of it, they had over 150 clients. It also proved perfect for the better work-life balance she had been seeking.

A very personal quest

Speaking of her inspiration for launching a website that offers a more holistic approach to healing, Sharda says: "For years I suffered from a debilitating migraine. I met neurologists, headache specialists, orthopaedists & GPs who, between them, put me on every possible drug combination. But the pain refused to budge. Finally, it was a simple diagnosis that worked: low levels of Vitamins B12 & D3. Within a few months of taking these simple, inexpensive supplements, I literally got a new life. Supplements have since helped my family work through their autoimmune disorders, without recourse to steroids or other long-term, side-effects-laden medication."

"Therein was born the idea for Sepalika (pronounced say-pah-li-ka, it is a fragrant night jasmine plant that is revered for its medicinal properties) – a website offering research-based healthcare advice on dietary supplements that enables people to just stay healthy or even manage the side effects of drugs."

Sharda speaks very highly of her Co-Founder, Mahesh Jayaraman. "I have never had anyone explain any illness with such lucidity, nor have I seen someone analyse lab reports so well. He connects the dots like no doctor I know. Not just me, my family and a host of folks have benefitted from his healing. Mahesh drives the content for Sepalika. We hope to use his incredible knowledge on health and medicine to help people live vibrantly."

Mahesh's interest in the field was driven also by a very personal experience. Mahesh's wife had a condition, which although not life-threatening was still quite serious, especially if it had not been detected early on. As the senior neurologist at the hospital was away at the time, she was entrusted into the care of a more junior doctor. Not only was she put through "a number of unnecessary and expensive tests", she was put on medication that was "too strong" for her condition. As a result, she had a bad reaction to the medication that caused one side of her body to become paralysed.

"With no explanations forthcoming from the bevvy of doctors billed to her care, I was forced to research the medicines and side effects online during the night, having been by her side all day long. I realised that most of us are not informed buyers of medical services," recalls Mahesh.

After a week-long ordeal, by which time the main neurologist had returned, Mahesh decided to take his wife home. She was taken off the strong medication and given a milder dose.

She steadily made a full recovery but the experience left a lasting impression on him.

Mahesh's interest in alternative medicine spurred him on to learn *Varmam*, magnet-based acupressure, NLP, Bach Flower Remedies, nutrition and Faster EFT. He uses a combination of all of these techniques to help clients regain their health. He also studied more conventional allopathic diagnostic techniques, including lab report analysis, understanding radiology reports, clinical diagnostic skills, etc.

Mahesh goes on to say, "In my opinion, as patients, we must all have the right information to take correct decisions on our medical treatment. Not all doctors have the time or knowledge or inclination to guide us. There is a very important role for a health counsellor who has the technical skills needed to simplify what's happening and guide us correctly – both on mainstream treatment and on alternative medicine choices."

A partnership based on shared beliefs and a common goal

Both Sharda and Mahesh come at the business with a shared interest in helping people address the root cause of their condition, rather than simply treating the symptoms with medication. They truly believe that they have an opportunity to create a "go-to site" where there is expertise and authority in the area of vitamins and supplements.

The journey to where they are today involved some trial and error. When they first embarked on the idea 18 months ago, they thought it would be an *Ayurvedic* website, before changing direction towards wholefoods and finally settling on dietary supplements.

The addressable market and existing competition

There is competition out there in the form of the likes of WebMD and Examine.com, but Sharda believes that through Sepalika there is an opportunity to create a community of practitioners, academic experts and users (such as the American Association of Retired Persons). The aim is to provide a research-based website that is more rigorous than "*daadima's* (grandma's) remedies" whilst being easy to understand from a consumer's point of view.

In the US alone, dietary supplements make up a market worth $30 billion, despite it not being covered by health insurance. Sharda believes this proves that customers want to take greater control of their own health, irrespective of insurance cover. She also believes that a healthier population is ultimately in the interests of the health insurance firms that could face lower claims for expensive medication and hospital treatment.

Monetising the opportunity and long-term vision

Is the purpose of the website mainly altruistic or do they envisage making money from it? And if so, how? "The aim is to make a profit but it is also about creating the greatest impact," say Sharda. They both firmly believe that the human body has an inherent ability to heal itself if it is given the chance to do so. The website launched in March 2016 and so the business is still in its infancy. Their prime focus now is to add interesting content on it and drive traffic on to it.

In terms of financing of the business, Sepalika has been fortunate to have found Venture Capital (VC) investors, who in exchange for equity in the business provide them with funding and invaluable advice on how to measure the success of a website-led business.

Sharda's long-term vision (five years plus) is to "make Sepalika the go-to resource to help people heal themselves and use dietary supplements to prevent disease, rather than rely on medication that is more like a life support".

Lessons learnt and advice

- "Being an entrepreneur requires a huge level of commitment."
- "Find investors who can also provide advice and be mentors."

"Learn to be flexible and open. Be willing to ask experts for advice. Have no egos."

Mumtrepreneurs: Mums who became homegrown entrepreneurs

Becoming a mother is a life-changing event. Whether or not a new mother goes back to work is not always a matter of choice. Many do because they cannot afford not to. But equally, mothers increasingly choose to work because they don't want to give up an identity that goes beyond being a mother.

When my husband offered to take on the role of the stay-at-home parent after the birth of our daughter, he was in a small minority. Nearly 16 years on, more men are choosing to play a prominent role in the raising of their children, with some even becoming full-time dads. Whether or not you have childcare support within your immediate family or from your partner, becoming a mother should not be the reason for a woman losing her individuality, her independence and connection with the outside world.

We are living in a time where advances in technology, the benefits of globalisation and better provision of childcare are making almost anything possible. Becoming a mother makes you more aware of time, or the lack of it. Many women who return to work after maternity leave are known to become fantastically productive with a laser-like focus, wasting no time in getting the job done so they can return home to their baby. Forward-thinking employers value these women for their loyalty and increased productivity.

Finding interesting things that lie beyond her immediate circle of responsibilities should be every woman's goal. Cultivating interests and hobbies from a young age has other advantages: it helps us to discover things about ourselves that might otherwise remain hidden. They also provide the perfect antidote for the mundaneness or stress of our everyday life.

Activities that enrich our minds and gainfully occupy our time can pay enormous dividends today and later in life. Some of the ladies whose stories you are about to read harnessed a talent or hobby into a micro-enterprise they could run on their own terms. Financial independence, doing things we love and loving the things we do, as well as having a network of supporters outside of our close family are aspects that can empower women, no matter how old they are or where they live in the world.

Women who spend their entire lives being a dutiful daughter, someone's wife, a loving mother and carer of elderly relatives do their families and society a huge service. If you know someone who fits that label, remember to let her know how much she is appreciated.

Women whose lives revolve around their children are more likely to find the empty nest syndrome hardest to bear. Our children will grow up and leave home some day. They may forever be our reason for living, but we must accept that when they find their own meaning in life it won't necessarily include us. We can but guide them and hope that in time they will confidently make their own way in the world with a partner in life, and with allies and mentors to support them along the way.

CHAPTER 24

Anusha Sodavaram
– Serial Entrepreneur
– The UK

Anusha's traditional upbringing did not stop her from exploring new opportunities through education and now her work. The encouragement of her parents and supportive husband has helped as she juggles full-time work, entrepreneurship and motherhood with equanimity and positivity.

Anusha grew up in a small town in India in a very traditional family. Despite her sheltered upbringing, her parents were very supportive of her desire to be independent. She moved alone to Delhi to study journalism. She recalls this being a big step for her to live in a big city that was a far cry from the close-knit and conservative society she had grown up in. After graduating, she worked for a while as a journalist and then moved into an internal communications role.

Becoming a foreign student

After Anusha got married, her husband encouraged her to pursue further education abroad. She enrolled into the two-year Erasmus Mundus European Journalism programme in Denmark. Any reservations she might have had about travelling alone for the first time to a non-English speaking country were quickly banished. She received a warm welcome at the university where she was amongst students of varying nationalities. In her quest to be financially independent, she took up a part-time job working at an Indian restaurant. In 2011, she won the Marjorie Deane scholarship so that she could complete the second year of the programme in London.

Despite her excellent qualifications, and perhaps because all her previous work experience had been in India, it took Anusha two and a half years to find a full-time job in a marketing role of her choice in London. She did various part-time roles during that time. Meanwhile, her husband also moved to London, and just as her career was starting to pick up, she discovered that she was expecting their first child.

Becoming a mumtrepreneur

At first, she had thought she would return to work at the end of her maternity leave and rely on the family for childcare help. But once her daughter was born she found the idea of leaving her each day to go back to a demanding full-time job simply did not appeal.

She had the option of staying on with her former employer in a marketing role on a contract basis (giving her more flexibility than a full-time role) but decided against it. She chose instead to go into catering because she thought it was something she could do from her home. She liked the idea of being her own boss and having the flexibility to be there for her daughter. Anusha's friends had always complimented her cooking and gave their support when she told them about her new idea.

A1 Meals was launched as a service that offers lunchtime meals to offices. She targeted the Indian community in offices, who were delighted at the prospect of home cooked Indian meals being delivered to their desks. She found clients by promoting her business on targeted Facebook groups. Once she had found her very first customer, a company in Central London, her clientele grew through recommendations.

Her daily routine was gruelling. She would wake up at 4am, prepare the meals for the day and carry them by public transport before lunchtime to where her clients were. Despite the success of the business, she found she was spending far too much time travelling and not enough with her daughter.

She decided to branch away from daily meals, which were time-consuming and low value because there is a limit to how much people will spend on their daily meals. After her brand and her name had become established in the Indian community, she was able to change direction and transition the business towards catering for events.

Rather than do this from her own kitchen, she found someone who had access to a commercial kitchen but no independent brand, and had all the relevant certifications needed to start cooking on a more industrial scale. Together they hired a team of people who worked when they were needed, cooking and delivering the food to the customer. Anusha remains the face of the business, taking care of its marketing, customer service and quality control, to ensure the service always meets her high standards.

Anusha personally contacts the customers after each event to ensure everything went well and to receive feedback. "The business has its ups and downs but the customer service is always the most important aspect of it," she says. Even when she has had unhappy customers, she has always managed to turn the situation around so that they have come back time and again.

Juggling business, a career and motherhood

With a new partner in the business and a team that took care of the operations, she found she had more time on her hands. Her daughter was thriving in a full-time pre-school where she benefited from the interaction with other children. Anusha decided she was ready to return to the corporate world and took on the role of Marketing Manager, which covers the UK, Europe and Asia. She still wakes up at 4am, leaves the house at 6am, and drives 130 kilometres by car to work and back before returning home to take care of her family. She has no hired home help and does most of the cooking and cleaning herself.

How does she do it: being in a full-time job, running a business, being a mum and also playing the role of a homemaker? "I have a really supportive husband," she says, who has always believed in her ability to do whatever she sets her mind to. They are both of the view that if you take on something, you need to give it 100 per cent or not do it at all.

Lessons learnt and advice

- "Do things for yourself."
- "Throw out negativity. Absorb positivity."

"Get a reality check: it is your life! Nobody owes you anything and you don't owe anyone anything."

CHAPTER 25

Dipali Koundinya – Franchisee, GlobalArt – India

Dipali gave up a corporate career to spend more time with her daughter. Not content to be just a housewife, she started art classes for children as a franchisee of a well recognised global brand and now has two centres and 250 students.

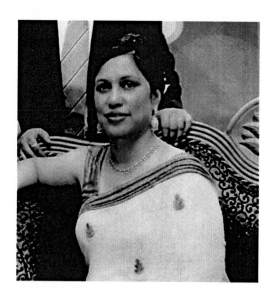

Dipali qualified as a software engineer in India. After she was married, she and her husband lived and worked in the US for a few years. They returned to India when their daughter was a year old and decided to settle in Bangalore. At first, she took on a full-time job working for accountancy giant Price Waterhouse Coopers (PWC) but found she barely saw her daughter because of the long hours she was putting in. When her daughter was about four years old, Dipali decided she wanted to spend more time being a mother and quit her job.

Franchisee route: a lower risk way to entrepreneurship

Art is something Dipali has always loved and she has pursued it as a hobby throughout her life. She was looking for suitable art classes for her daughter in Bangalore when she came across GlobalArt. Dipali was attracted to the idea that they had a curriculum that encourages creativity, as she did not want to see her daughter's creativity stifled by teachers who were too structured and sought to impose their own style on their students. Dipali discovered that GlobalArt had a few centres in Bangalore but none were close enough to where she lived.

GlobalArt was established in 1999 in Malaysia as a way of using art and creative drawing as tools to enhance a child's mental faculties, broaden their imagination and help them to explore hidden creative talent. It is now an international franchise with its programme being implemented across 15 countries with 600 centres and more than a million learners worldwide.

Dipali was encouraged by friends and family to start her own centre as a franchisee. Although setting up on her own was a daunting challenge, the parent company was very supportive and she got plenty of advice and rigorous training to help her on her way. As a franchisee, her initial investment was in the form of a franchise fee and the cost of hiring the venue where she would hold the classes.

The franchising route is an excellent way to set up your own business whilst piggybacking on an established brand, a proven product or service and a network of people who have done it before and give you centralised back up.

Her first centre was in an apartment complex where she rented a place. She created awareness of her new classes by launching art competitions in schools (with the winner getting a free place) and doing art workshops as free taster sessions. She also used the local newspapers to advertise the opening of her art centre.

The GlobalArt curriculum targets children aged 5 to 15 and so mainly offers afterschool programmes that students typically attend once a week. There are different levels of teaching offered that depend on age group and the levels of achievement, with children receiving certification at the end of each level.

Dipali was pleased with the level of response she got but was also very aware of the need to create an environment where "all the stakeholders were happy and remained interested". To ensure the children did not get bored, she added other things such as arts and crafts, designing and other related classes in addition to the prescribed GlobalArt curriculum.

She is also part of another franchise that focuses on art teaching for adults.

Successfully growing the niche

Dipali now has two centres with 250 children attending her classes and 10 people working for her, including a Centre Manager who takes care of the administration and human resources functions. Most of her employees are women and have come to her as a result of referrals. Candidates who apply don't need to be artists themselves but they must be able to relate well to children. Being able to communicate with children in the right way is far more important than any other qualification. After she has vetted them, the candidates need corporate approval from the Indian head office in Chennai before she can employ them.

In terms of competitors, there are numerous individuals who teach from apartment complexes or from their own homes, but there are no corporate competitors of the same ilk as GlobalArt in India. This partly explains why the pricing of her services is higher than more traditional art classes. But it does not pose a problem for Dipali as parents who choose to go with GlobalArt do so in the knowledge that "it is not a regular art programme" and justifies paying extra.

What have been the rewards for Dipali of turning a hobby into a business? Other than giving her the opportunity to quit corporate life and take greater control of her own working life, she enjoys the beneficial impact that her art classes have on her students. "Sometimes parents have come back to me to say that their children's concentration and handwriting has improved since they started attending my classes." Even in instances where parents had initially complained about the high fees, they have later admitted that it has been worth the added expense.

Has Dipali found the work-life balance she was seeking? "When I first started I had to spend a lot of time working, but it was worth it." Now that she has a system in place and a reliable team of people who work for her, she has found a better work-life balance. She believes that the very personal connection she maintains with all the stakeholders in her business (the children, her employees and the parents) is at the root of her success.

Does she get to interact with other franchisees in the business? "Every year there is a national level art competition and they invite franchisees to speak." These events are meant to bring together people from around the country, so franchisees can share experiences and motivate one another. The art competition is also a healthy way to promote excellence at an individual centre level and motivates the children to give it their best.

Long-term vision

Dipali loves her work as part of GlobalArt and it continues to be the most important driver of her business. Her long-term vision is to work with children, but not just in the field of art. "Today's generation of young people is too pampered, spend too much time on gadgets. I want to have a place where children can explore their creativity and communicate with other children," says Dipali.

Lessons learnt and advice

- "The most important things are your ability and willingness to take a risk and jump in."
- "Have confidence in yourself to see things through."

"Having a supportive family and network of friends is helpful, but ultimately it is up to you."

CHAPTER 26

Inez Robinson
– Serial Entrepreneur
– Spain

Inez has battled adversity throughout her life. She is one of life's triers with a number of entrepreneurship experiments under her belt. In recent years, she has finally found stability and success in both her personal and working life.

Inez is a serial entrepreneur and her philosophy has always been: "If you don't enjoy what you do, then it's time for a change."

When Inez was a youngster growing up in the UK her father had ambitions for her to become a doctor. But in her late teens, Inez suffered an accident and discovered she could not stand the sight of blood, which effectively ended any notion of her becoming a doctor.

A passion for property development

Inez discovered she had a natural flair for property development and became responsible for dealing with tenants and helping her employer to grow their property portfolio. From this, she moved into mortgages and found she enjoyed the interaction with people. The market was strong (thanks to a booming UK property market) and it gave her the confidence to set up her own company in 1989. Unfortunately, it proved to be the top of the property cycle and a year later she was declared bankruptcy.

In the following few years, Inez had two children. Having found it difficult to get a job that suited her, she decided instead to study law. She remembers being interviewed for work experience by two women who were lawyers. "We were getting along really well but their attitude completely changed when they realised I had two children. The women clearly thought a career in law did not sit well with being a mother."

At around the same time Inez and her husband were considering moving to Australia with their two children. They were persuaded to move to Spain instead, where her parents had a villa. She decided to drop her plans to pursue a career in law that would geographically limit where she could practice.

Within two years of moving to Spain Inez's first marriage ended. In 1995, she discovered an opportunity to work as a children's entertainer for birthday parties and similar events, doing both face painting and magic. Although enjoyable, it involved working weekends and by the time she ended that venture eight years later she was exhausted. During that period she had also started a telemarketing business.

Inez later discovered there was a gap in the market for property auctions, and launched her business in 2003, when the Spanish economy was booming. She was on the verge of franchising her business to cover other parts of Spain in 2006 when the market nosedived and she was once again facing real financial hardship. It was a rocky time for Inez, who was in poor health as a result of the financial stress and a breakdown of her second marriage.

Happiness and stability at last

Inez met her current husband, Patrick, around this time and then came across Herbalife, a company that specialises in nutrition supplements and weight management products. She was invited to a presentation that really opened her eyes to what network marketing was all about. She heard success stories and testimonials from women working for

Herbalife, who had achieved things they could not have done by themselves.

She and Patrick became distributors in 2008 and have never looked back. At first, she discovered the selling process was very different to anything she had done before. "I found the idea of talking to complete strangers (about my products) terrifying," she remembers. Inez was surprised to find that a number of people were aware of the brand and had at some point in their lives used their products. This made converting them to customers, and even potential recruits, easier. It started from humble beginnings, when Inez and Patrick had their first sampling event and invited friends and people in the community, but they now have a stable income and an established base of customers and recruits.

Lessons learnt and advice

"The right opportunities will open up for you so long as you have the right attitude and a good work ethic."

CHAPTER 27

Ruchi Manipal – Founder, Palchin Photography – The UK

Ruchi gave up a successful career in marketing when she had her daughter. Her move into professional photography, covering birthdays, weddings and other special events, has enabled her to turn a passion into a profession.

Ruchi is an MBA from India where she had a successful career in marketing, initially with the online recruitment firm Monster.com and then in wealth management at ICICI and then HSBC.

After she got married she moved to London to be with her husband. Despite her previous experience in wealth management, she was unsuccessful in getting a similar role in London. The timing may not have helped; it was 2008 with the financial sector and the UK economy in considerable turmoil.

Eventually, Ruchi got a job in telecoms doing digital marketing and promotions. She remained in this job for about three years before leaving to have a baby. Once her daughter was born she had no desire to go back to full-time working and wanted to find something that she could do on her own terms.

Turning a passion into a profession

Ruchi had always been a keen amateur photographer. She loved the entire process of taking pictures, downloading them and editing them. She realised that she could be doing this professionally when she compared her own work to that done by some professional photographers.

She contacted a local events organiser and offered to do a couple of events for free, as a way to start building a portfolio. "Every event manager can have two or three photographers on their books, and so you may end of competing on price because it is not always possible to demonstrate you are that much better than the others", Ruchi tells me. The trial was very successful and it gave her the confidence to go out and start marketing her services directly.

At first, she started with "a very basic Nikon" camera and charged very little for her services. She wanted to learn with every shot. "When you are shooting pictures of others there is more pressure. It is very different to when you do it for yourself," says Ruchi. From such humble beginnings, she built herself a base of happy clients who told others about her work. She thinks 60-70 per cent of her work now comes from word of mouth.

Her initial investment into the business was modest. Other than her Nikon, there was the expense of paying for editing software (Adobe Photoshop and Lightroom), as well as the cost of a studio and props. As business picked up, she invested in a higher-end camera and better lenses. After her first year of being a professional photographer, Ruchi found she had bookings at least a month in advance.

Targeted marketing using social media

In terms of marketing, other than word of mouth recommendations, her main source of new business is via social media, although she also plans to have her own website soon. She has chosen to target mainly Asians in the UK because Ruchi feels she understands their culture, making it easier for her to build a rapport with them.

It is now two years since Ruchi founded Palchin. Although it was meant to help her achieve a better work-life balance whilst being a mother, she admits that she is taking on far more work than she had originally planned. "Photography is very time-consuming: it is a full-time job if you want to do it professionally." Marketing, going to events, waiting times, the actual time spent taking photos and the editing of the work are all things that "can take over your personal life," she warns.

Key to success: happy customers

Ruchi contacts her customers before the event and has a detailed conversation about the event itself: what the customer wants in terms of who should be in the pictures, in what setting, etc. In her view, her relationship with her clients is the most important reason why she wins business. "People don't pick a photographer purely on the quality of the photographs."

Has Ruchi ever had an unhappy customer and how did she deal with the situation? She recalls one client who had hired her for a party. In the pre-event conversation, the lady had been very clear about what she wanted from Ruchi. But when she got the final results she was not too happy because the full length of her dress had not been captured in any of the photos. Ruchi was able to respectfully point out that it was not one of the things that had been discussed when she had laid out what she wanted from the pictures. But it taught her a valuable lesson: you sell clients what they want but you must also give them what they need. And knowing what the latter is makes all the difference.

Another time, Ruchi was doing a photo-shoot in a studio for a family when about two-thirds of the way through her camera inexplicably stopped working. She apologised profusely and even though the customer was happy with what she had shot until that point, she offered them a second mini-shoot for free on another date.

This customer-centric approach and attention to detail are some of the reasons why Palchin Photography continues to win new customers, despite it being in a competitive field, and why they go on to recommend Ruchi's services to friends and family.

Lessons learnt and advice

- "Your relationship with your client is the most important success factor."
- "You have to be passionate about photography."
- "It cannot just be about the money."

"As a photographer, I always remind myself that women love getting dressed up for special occasions and when they do, they want a permanent memory of what they were wearing and how they looked."

CHAPTER 28

Sonal Sher – Founder, Eindie – The UK

Eindie is a very personal quest by Sonal to bring the best of Indian and English flavours together in the form of memorable homemade chutneys and relishes. She currently runs her business from home, whilst also working part-time and looking after her two children.

Sonal is a trained chef and cooking has always been a passion for her. She is also the mother of two boys and the need for a better work-life balance led her to reconsider her own career choices.

She founded Lunch Angels, a corporate gourmet business that served up tasty pre-ordered lunches to businesses for their corporate meetings. That idea was borne out of her own dreary experience with the same old soggy fare that was served up during corporate lunches in her previous working life in Retail and Hospitality.

Lunch Angels had a promising start but, by its very nature, is a more time critical and demanding business, and she found it harder to fit around her responsibilities. So she has put that venture on the backburner and decided instead to focus on something that she could work on in her own time and from home.

Targeting a new niche

Sonal had been making chutneys and selling them on an informal basis for a few years, mainly to her network of friends and other mums from her boys' school. She sold over 100 jars the first time she made them. She had always known making handmade chutneys would be a separate business to Lunch Angels. As a businesswoman, she had to take a decision about which one to of the two to focus on and better fitted in with her lifestyle. Her initial sales were entirely based on word of mouth endorsements and repeat orders.

Encouraged by the feedback she got from her early customers she decided to create a brand that was representative of herself: a person of Indian origin who now lives in the UK. She was clear that the brand would be linked with a "product that was me", modern and different to what is available on supermarkets shelves. It would be Indian but with a twist; flavours that blend beautifully the best of Indian and British tastes, such as sweet red onion marmalade with hints of nutmeg. She currently makes the chutneys in her own kitchen.

Her brand Eindie (E for English ad Indie for Indian) was launched in March 2016 in the presence of a number of local dignitaries and friends at Tante Marie, which is also a Culinary Academy. Sonal has a clear vision of where the brand can go. The labelling and the packaging had to be "modern, clean and minimalistic", allowing the complex flavours inside to do the talking.

The price point for her chutneys and relishes was determined by testing out many similar products already in the market. It is targeted at a local customer base that appreciates handmade products and is willing to pay a premium for it. She admits that it is a crowded market with lots of competition. However, Sonal is convinced there is a profitable niche for handmade products that are tasty and make cooking a more pleasurable experience for her customers.

Juggling act

She currently also works four days a week in a job that gives her financial security, the flexibility to be there for her two children and time to work on Eindie. She loves the fact that her free time is being spent on something that she is passionate about and that it could be the start of something a lot bigger. Sonal admits that she would need to spend a lot more time on Eindie if she was to take it to a scale where it could be sufficiently profitable.

Over her career, she has made excellent contacts in the culinary world and knows people who could help her manufacture her chutneys on a more commercial scale. However, she needs to find a way to maintain the exclusivity of the product being handmade, whilst still producing it in commercial quantities.

Sonal's vision for Eindie

Two of Sonal's key missions are to help change the perception of how chutneys can be used and to broaden their appeal. She uses the tagline "flavour infusions" on her creations. Her products have a shelf life of at least a year and can be used to add an exciting twist to whatever dish one might be cooking – be it a humble lentil "*daal*" or even a pasta sauce.

Apart from selling direct to order within her local community, she has four flavours of her chutneys stocked for sale at a local wine bar on Woking High Street called Cellar Magneval. She intends to sell online too, but only in bulk. She understands the importance of continued access to customer feedback, especially once she has ceded control of that direct link to retailers. In due course, she plans to create a website for Eindie and use social media to create communities of customers so they can share experiences and menus on how they used their relishes in their cooking.

Eindie is a labour of love and Sonal wants to ensure she gives it the best chance of success by focusing on product quality, brand image, deliverability and customer satisfaction.

Lesson learnt and advice

- "If you are in the UK, go to your local council for advice and access to a mentor on starting up your own business."
- "Get yourself an accountant/tax adviser. Use someone who has recently qualified and so will know enough to help you, but will not be as expensive as the bigger firms."

"Don't be rigid with your business plan, especially in the early days. Prepare to be fluid."

CHAPTER 29

Swapna Karpe
– Founder, Sugar 'n' Spice
Cakery – The USA

After spending over a decade as a homemaker and mother, when she enjoyed cooking and baking, Swapna has finally taken the plunge and set up her own bakery. This focuses on giving customers cakes that taste even more wonderful than they look.

Swapna qualified as a Haematologist in India but never really had a chance to pursue it as a career because she moved to the USA soon after getting married. Having two children within a short space of time and a husband who travelled extensively on business put any career plans on the backburner.

Taking the plunge and acquiring a taste for business

Swapna has always enjoyed baking and has been making cakes for friends and family for years. Over the past year, she has felt ready to take the next big step and turn it into a business. Her husband encouraged her to take the plunge. She got to grips with all the rules and regulations of setting up a food business from home. She believes what makes her cakes different is how they taste, not just how they look.

Did Swapna have a mentor who guided her through the early steps of setting up on her own? Although not exactly a mentor, Swapna sought inspiration from a friend who is herself an entrepreneur and has pioneered an event called the *Desi Mela* that provides a platform for women of Indian origin who are also entrepreneurs. Swapna recently took part in this event where her cake stall sat alongside others displaying *sarees*, handmade jewellery and other exotic Indian specialities. It was a resounding success and gave her young business exactly the sort of exposure and impetus it needed.

She has also found a good support system in her local Mom's Club who were very helpful when she was new to the community. Swapna is a believer in collaborations and helping one another and so is part of both formal and informal networks of friends of fellow female entrepreneurs who share ideas and promote each other's businesses.

Swapna tells me that food safety rules in the USA mean she cannot cook anything else in her kitchen whilst she is baking cakes for her business. Clearly, this can be tricky when you also have a family to feed. Fortunately, the family is hugely supportive of Swapna's venture and her husband and children help out in whatever way they can, "Even if it means eating takeout food whilst mom is busy with baking."

Target customer, competition and innovation

Given the perishable nature of the goods, Swapna primarily targets a local customer base. But she is not averse to taking orders from elsewhere for products with a longer shelf life and where the order size is large enough to justify postage charges.

Her target customer base mainly comprises the Indian community in the Philadelphia area where she lives and her business is based. She does little in the way of traditional advertising, as most of her business is generated through recommendations and word of mouth, and uses social media and Facebook groups that cover her local Asian community to post her adverts.

Swapna is building brand awareness by participating in fairs and events that have the right location and suitable demographic of attendees. She has discovered that it is much better to have a stall in fairs that is aimed at families because children are more likely to want to sample her cakes, which can subsequently result in a sale. Swapna also has a website where she displays a range of her cake offerings along with a pricing guide. She charges extra for any personalisation or customised themes.

Swapna firmly believes that great customer service is the key to success. If a customer is unhappy, she always tries to understand why and to appease them if possible. She requests feedback from her customers, either directly or via her FB page.

How does she view the competition? Swapna accepts that there are many bakeries like hers but what really matters is the end product. "Every baker will impart their own unique flavour and style to their cakes. The feedback on my cakes is that they are fresh, moist and not too sweet. And I always aim to make them the day before delivery."

Swapna is driven by innovation. "I'm doing a lot of research on tastes and flavours," says Swapna. For the *Desi Mela,* she came up with a new line of flavours for her cupcakes that captured some international delicacies, such as Indian *Gulab Jamans*, Turkish *Baklava* and Mexican *Chilli*. "The *Gulab Jaman* and the *Baklava* flavoured cupcakes were rated very highly" and has spurred her on to try some more exotic flavours in time for the Indian festival of lights (and eating copious quantities of sweet), *Diwali* later in the year.

Long-term vision

How does Swapna cope with sudden spurts in demand? Whilst her business is still in its start-up phase she does not have enough work to hire someone on a permanent basis, but she envisages using someone on a flexible basis. If business picks up on a sustained basis then she has the option of converting some additional space in her house into a kitchen that will become a dedicated bakery. It will require investment in new kit and other fittings, but it will offer much greater flexibility.

Lesson learnt and advice

"Don't think too much about it, just do it. The worst that can happen is that you fail."

Givers: social enterprise and philanthropy

Search for meaning in life

As a society, we have made significant economic progress resulting in innovation, wealth creation and greater leisure time for many. At the same time, our society has become very achievement orientated; one that adores successful and happy people, and in particular the young. It virtually ignores the value of all those who are otherwise. We are living in an era where value equates to the present usefulness of an individual.

When viewed through this narrow prism of what one's life is worth, is it surprising that there are so many who are unhappy and feel worthless, and yet feel compelled to put on a happy facade? News of seemingly happy and content people "with everything to live for" taking their own lives is greeted with puzzlement and deep sadness. At the other end of the spectrum, we are awestruck and amazed at stories of survivors of unimaginable hardship and suffering, debilitating illnesses and life-changing accidents when death might have seemed a preferred option to an impartial observer.

Man's Search For Meaning by Viktor E Frankl's is a gem of a book that changed the way I viewed my own life when I first read it in the summer of 2015. Who better to explore the way the human mind works and what causes us to behave the way we do than a man who survived four concentration camps, including the most infamous of them all Auschwitz, and one who was a psychotherapist by profession.

The author's experiences and anecdotes from his camp life show us that man does have a choice of actions, even in the face of the most terrible circumstances. He may choose to retain his human dignity and inner freedom despite the dehumanising conditions he is subjected to day after day. "The way in which a man accepts his fate and all the suffering it entails, the way in which he takes up his cross, gives him ample opportunity, even under the most difficult circumstances, to add a deeper meaning to his life."

Finding individual meaning in life, what each of us can bring to life, rather than always questioning what life has in store for us, is but the first step to collectively forming a more responsible and empathetic society.

The power of empathy

We live in a deeply unequal world. Never has the divide between the haves and have-nots been wider. At the same time, we are in a highly connected and informed world with access to real-time information at our fingertips. Technology has made it possible to connect people from around the globe, share stories, drive change and make a difference.

Giving has little to do with what you start out with, notably in terms of material things. A kind word costs nothing but could change someone's life for the better. Giving is about empathy and compassion. Empathy is not just a fluffy trait in the gift of do-gooders. We are all probably born with it but don't always recognise it or remember to practice it. Like most of nature's gifts, it needs to be recognised for what it is worth and nurtured.

I practise it with my children and they sometimes think I can read their minds. Amazing how easy it is to know what someone is thinking when you put yourself in their shoes. I have used it with great success in my working life: in meetings with complete strangers to break the ice and put them at ease; during formal presentations when a part of you temporarily leaves your body to watch yourself from the eyes of your audience and recognises that you are losing them (a cue to change tack or lose them forever). Empathy even made me a better investor because it is the stone that sharpens your sixth sense, better known as instinct, and provides that extra secret sauce that cannot be explained and is best not revealed.

Empathy makes you more interested in the other person's point of view, their vision and what makes them tick. It makes you a kinder colleague, a better parent, a more understanding friend, as well as a more tolerant and loving spouse. But above all, being empathetic just makes sense because nothing bad ever came from it and plenty of good did.

As parents we play a very important role in helping our children see the world, not just through their own eyes, but also through the prism of someone else's experiences, starting with the school playground. Teach them to spot that one child who is always alone and friendless. Making them think about how lonely and sad that child must feel, and then doing their bit to change that. Bringing up our children to become more empathetic and kind is one of the greatest gifts we can give this world.

You will now read stories of five women and a man (who told me the story of his late mother, whose giver genes live on in him). They each found their respective calling that has either come from a deeply personal experience, or out of sheer compassion for a section of society that has been overlooked. They are united in their aim: to make society more aware and inclusive, and to equip disadvantaged people in the community to become independent, productive and engaged members of society.

CHAPTER 30

Anna Kennedy OBE – Founder, Anna Kennedy Online – The UK

When Anna realised over two decades ago that the British education system was failing her two boys, she decided to set up her own school for autistic children. That was the start of a very personal crusade to raise awareness and inclusion of children with autism both in the UK and around the world.

Anna has two sons, Patrick and Angelo. Her eldest son, Patrick, did not have an easy start to life. He was born premature, suffered complications during birth and was in and out of hospital a lot in the early years. The family had access to a psychotherapist to help them deal with the stress of it all.

A double blow

As Patrick was growing up he hated school and so getting him there was a monumental struggle every single morning. "The number of times I nearly crashed my car because he was having a meltdown," remembers Anna. Her younger son Angelo was two years old when he was diagnosed with autism. It was only then that they discovered that Patrick, aged six, also had a related condition called Asperger's. Patrick had in fact been diagnosed with it when he was four years old, but the authorities had not told his parents.

How did Anna and her husband react to this information? "At first, we looked for reasons to blame. We had no support at all, found no strategies to be followed. It was like we were dealing with a huge minefield," says Anna. Did it help that she could now explain why her boys behaved the way they did? "My sons were the same but now they had a label. This was back in 1996-97 – there wasn't much known about autism other than what we had seen in 'Rain Man' (the movie starring Dustin Hoffman)." Anna's memory of that time is tinged with a sense of isolation. Her family was based in the North East of England, whilst she was in London with her husband and boys.

Anna found out about the UK charity, the National Autistic Society and finally got in touch with them after a few unsuccessful attempts. They sent her a video that was meant to give her information about people with autism, but instead it featured children and people with the most severe form of autism. "I found it so depressing that I could not watch it through and I think I just buried it in the back of car boot or something." The hardest part was the not knowing what being autistic meant for her sons' future.

Educating her boys

Anna wanted to keep her boys in a mainstream education system, ideally in a normal school with a special unit attached to it that could cater to her boys' needs. But it became increasingly clear to her that the schools were simply not equipped to cater for Patrick's or Angelo's needs and so they were turned away from 26 schools.

Anna had no choice but to embark on homeschooling for her two sons. With Patrick being entitled to five hours a week of lessons, she converted their garage into a classroom, but Angelo's condition was more severe. The teacher who came to teach him found she did not have the right expertise. "She was a lovely lady but broke down in tears after three days because she just didn't know how to get through to Angelo."

Anna soon realised that the homeschooling option was not working. Five hours a week for Patrick was not enough and Angelo needed specialist attention. "When I get a bee in my bonnet, I am unstoppable," says Anna of her efforts to do something that no other parent of a child with autism in the

UK had ever dared to do. She decided it was time to set up her own school. Anna had met with another parent who was also coping with a child on the spectrum and she found her first ally in her.

Starting a specialist school and the kindness of strangers

Anna and her husband started the school building project from their lounge with a small support group that quickly grew to 275 strong. "It was a huge learning curve; I did lots of reading." Among the many things she had to do early on was contacting the Department of Education so that she was complying with their rules, sourcing funds from the bank to build the school and finding a suitable Head Teacher. They had heard about a local school that was scheduled to be demolished. Anna's husband helped her to create both a business plan and feasibility study to convert it into a school for autistic children. They then remortgaged their home and used every penny of their savings to raise the funds.

Sadly, big organisations that dealt with children with autism were unwilling to share information with Anna and there were many doubters. But her uncompromising attitude and determination to do the best for her boys and others like them won her support, sometimes from the most unexpected of quarters.

Anna turned to her local community for help. She approached the Probation Service, who sent offenders to volunteer and work on the building site. It was particularly heart-warming that even after their community service time was up, some of them returned as volunteers. British Airways sent a group of their employees on a team building exercise there and built the school kitchen. "Volunteers started coming out of the woodwork to help us, including carpenters, painters and electricians."

A labour of love that bears fruit

Anna had planned on completing the project within three years, but they finished it in just 18 months. The viability of the school also depended on other parents being willing to send their children to her new school. "The hardest bit was the (education and children's services regulator) OFSTED regulation. A month after the school's opening, OFSTED came to inspect the school. They could have shut us down (if they had not been happy with the school) meaning that we would lose everything." Happily, things went swimmingly. So much so the inspector's parting words to Anna were that if he had a child with autism, he would have had no hesitation sending him or her to Anna's school.

Without a formal background in education, how did Anna know what a specialist school for children with autism should offer? "I knew what I wanted for my boys: a school as close to mainstream as possible with specialist support." Having the right Head Teacher was the most important factor, as they would run the school and turn Anna's vision into reality. In that sense, it was the most important post. "The Head Teacher we recruited was the very last person I interviewed and I just knew she was right for the job." The successful candidate had 17 years of experience, "knew what she was doing" and "followed an eclectic approach". Based on the needs of each individual student, she would adopt an approach that worked best and hire therapists for the school so we were not beholden to others. One of the things she did early on was to recruit a speech therapist who could provide valuable early input to children with delayed speech and language skills.

How did Anna ensure the school had enough funding to support her ambitious plan to provide specialist education? "When the school first started we didn't have all the funding we needed, but as it grew and added more children, we got more funding. Each child who joined the school came with a statement of special needs accompanied by a pot of funding from the government. The biggest bill at the school is staffing, but other resources, such as the equipment, are also expensive."

Expanding the scope and the reach

The school expanded its scope to cater for the growing needs and the progression of its students. For instance, after-school activities were added to the normal curriculum, so that the children did not miss out on this important aspect of school life.

Hillingdon Manor School in Uxbridge opened in 1999 with 19 students. Today, it is the largest of its kind in Europe, offering 180 autistic children a safe, structured education and a brighter future.

Buoyed by the success of the school and recognising that there was still a significant unmet need, Anna went on to set up two community colleges, a respite home for adults with autism, a second specialist school in Kent and the charity Anna Kennedy Online, which provides advice for parents who have children with autism. The website now also has a significant international following.

Engendering greater inclusion into society

The community colleges are open to people with autism from the ages of 16 to 59. The inclusion of older people is a deliberate nod to the fact that many children with autism will have missed out on an education and are ill prepared to become productive earning members of society. Better late than never.

The smaller of the two colleges provides more intensive one-to-one support, including teaching independent living skills to its students who tend to be more profoundly autistic. The other college actively seeks apprenticeships for its students. Anna knows that it can be difficult to get employers to be open to the prospect of employing someone with autism. But there is progress. "One of our graduates has got a job with Goldman Sachs," she tells me with pride.

The residential home is a safe place for adults with autism and currently has eight residents. It is used as a temporary home for when residents are taught independent living skills and can also provide a useful glimpse into the employability of those individuals.

Anna also "wanted to create something different", which led to the launch of initiatives such as Autism's Got Talent, a talent show for people with autism, and Give Us A Break, a national campaign to tackle bullying of children with autism in the playground or during break times. Anna is a regular speaker at events relating to autism and provides training to the likes of NSPCC and Childline on the issue of bullying and the use of social media by children on the spectrum.

Initiatives like Autism's Got Talent are Anna's way of showing the world that people with autism are no different from others in being creative, talented and seeking simply to live a normal life. Many autistic people find it hard to make friends and suffer social exclusion. "It is also about what happens behind the scenes; friendships develop and they keep in contact with each other."

Anna's life is devoted to her boys and to the greater cause of helping those with autism in the UK, and around the world. "I can't ever let my guard down," she admits and is quite accustomed to "never having an uninterrupted night's sleep" always listening out for her boys, in particular her younger son Angelo. She tells me about how Angelo recently went for a three-night trip with his group at community college: his first time ever away from home. "It felt very strange, the house was so quiet and I got to watch TV with no interruptions," she tells me. Patrick recently got an apprenticeship and hopes to get a permanent job soon.

Lessons learnt and advice

- "If your child is diagnosed with autism, start working with them as early as possible. It can be three steps forward and two steps back. Never give up hope. Fight for everything."

- In the UK, Free Schools (like the one Anna set up) are popular but "it is important to get the right team: a tight group with the right skills".

"Starting a school is not easy. You need a lot of funding to start and run a school. You need to have everything in place but even after all of that, if you don't pass the OFSTED test you can be closed down."

CHAPTER 31

Avril Hitman
– Founder, Magpie Dance
Company – The UK

Avril founded Magpie Dance Company over 30 years ago because she wanted to make dance more inclusive for people with learning disabilities. She genuinely believes that it is up to society to find a way of including differently abled people, rather than excluding them because of their disability.

Avril wanted to be a ballerina from the age of four when she started taking ballet lessons. As she got older she recognised that although she still enjoyed ballet very much, she did not believe she had the required skill to perform on stage. She decided to train to become a dance teacher instead, so she could share her love of dance with others.

In 1975 Avril enrolled herself into a teacher's training programme that enabled her to teach different genres of dance. After completing this she taught in schools, dance studios, helped students prepare for ballet exams and choreographed dances for festivals. Avril also taught adult ballet, an experience she thoroughly enjoyed.

Finding a new purpose

After ten years of teaching, Avril decided she needed a new challenge and started looking into the possibility of teaching people with learning difficulties, as she was aware that they enjoyed very few opportunities in the creative arts fields. SHAPE was an organisation that worked with people who had physical and learning challenges. They put her in touch with Wolfgang Stange of the Amici Dance Company in London.

Gina Levette, who founded Shape, asked Wolfgang to run movement sessions at Normansfield Hospital, the long-stay institution for people with severe learning difficulties. Wolfgang's success was such that he was soon teaching classes to groups with learning and/or physical difficulties in a range of venues. These sometimes included aspiring dancers without obvious disabilities. In 1980 he formed AMICI Dance Theatre Company and it made its ground-breaking debut at the London Roof Top Theatre. Wolfgang is now known internationally for his teaching methods, which stress the need to share and acknowledge each other's abilities, whether disabled or not.

Avril went to meet Wolfgang so that she could shadow him in his classes. She found the experience "overwhelming". During her second such visit, Avril accepted Wolfgang's offer to join in. "It was like an out of body experience," says Avril. She had the strongest feeling that "this is what I was meant to do."

"Individuals can put up a wall when they don't want you to see what they are thinking or feeling, so there's an element of pretence. But with people with learning disabilities, what you see is what you get. There is honesty and integrity; if they don't want to be there, they will say so."

Now that she had found her new challenge and purpose in life, she set about finding places where she could teach. She worked for health authorities, special schools, social service centres and community venues. She started volunteering on the condition that if they liked her work they would pay her for her time, especially as it was a job that involved a fair amount of responsibility.

Avril started working with the Astley Centre, a day centre run by social services for people with learning disabilities. At first, Avril worked alone but soon realised she needed volunteers to help her. Shirley, the mother of one of the attendees at the centre, became a volunteer and went on to work with Avril for the next seven years.

The group, comprising of 10 adults with learning disabilities, was called The Astley Dance Group. From 1985 to 1992, Avril ran it with two volunteers, exploring movement concepts and encouraging people to express themselves creatively. Bromley Mencap sponsored the sessions for the first six months and then The Astley Centre supported it. After several years at the Astley Centre, the sessions moved to the 'Magpie Youth Club', which is where the name Magpie Dance developed in the 1990s.

Making dance inclusive

Avril's aim from the outset was to encourage all people, regardless of their ability, to take a full and integrated part in the artistic life of the community. Thirty years ago, there was very little creative arts activity that people of any age with learning disabilities could participate in, let alone opportunities to perform.

Magpie's values and approach were founded on the social model of disability: *it is up to society to find a way of including people, rather than excluding because of disability*. Since the beginning, the aim was for the dancers to have as many opportunities as possible to perform and collaborate with different companies and artists. This remains vital to Magpie today.

What are the skills required to teach dance to those with learning disabilities? "You just have to be open-minded, tap into their creativity and be flexible. You need to have open expectations, don't close them down." When teaching people with special needs, all Avril wants to know is if there are any health issues that she needs to be aware of. Other than that, "I don't want to prejudge them. I believe that anything is possible. You just need to have self-belief. Having a disability should not preclude you from achieving great things."

How long did Avril have to work for nothing before her services were appreciated and paid for? "For the first six months, I was working for free as a volunteer, then started to get sponsorship from Bromley MENCAP who paid me for an hour and a half of teaching per week, and then got some funding from Social Services."

Avril admits that she was very fortunate to have had the wholehearted support of her family, given how much time she was spending away from home for so little money. "You need to have the buy-in from your nuclear family. My husband, my children and my parents never once missed a performance done by the Magpie students."

Initially, the sessions were all done in-house at the Astley Centre. The rest of the week Avril worked on a freelance basis and continued to do so until 2006. During this time she worked in community centres and special schools to gain further experience. She also continued to develop her skills by going on courses. "Going on practical courses helped but learning on the job was the most valuable." Avril estimates that 80 per cent of her learning is done on the job and she is still learning. "When you get to a time you think you have stopped learning, that is the time to stop."

In 1992, seven years after Magpie had its origins, Avril decided to start classes in the community. She really wanted to have them integrated with people without disabilities, but had limited success. "Perhaps I didn't market it very well," she says. The focus of Magpie is now entirely on people with learning disabilities and their support networks.

An unexpected windfall

"You have to grow something when it is ready to grow. Because Magpie had no funding (from the government) everything we do needs to be fundraised for." In 1994, Avril had an opportunity to apply for funding from the Foundation of Sport and the Arts, run by the Littlewoods Pools. "I had no experience of fundraising. My motto has always been to think big and not compromise on quality, especially when it comes to working with people who have learning disabilities," says Avril, as she explains why she asked for an ambitious £200,000 over a period of five years, not really expecting to be granted the whole amount. To her utter amazement, a letter arrived in the post one Saturday morning several months later, offering her £40,000 that had to be spent within a year as specified by the Foundation with the remaining tranches to follow in the following four years.

The grant enabled Avril to mount a hugely successful Gala evening at The Churchill Theatre in collaboration with the renowned Candoco Dance Company and the Jiving Lindy Hoppers. Magpie dancers performed to an audience of over 500 people. There were also guest performances and a live band on stage. Avril remembers the occasion being well received by the members of the audience.

Following the grant in 1994, Magpie was established as a Company Limited by Guarantee in 1996, and as a registered charity in 1997. During this decade, there was no central office base and no regular funding.

Building a legacy

The community classes became so popular they 'outgrew' the original session at Bromley and a second session was opened in Orpington in 2000. Furthermore, the education residencies in schools across the country increased year on year.

Magpie's early focus had been exclusively on adults with learning disabilities. "We realised that working with adults did not create a legacy. We started doing projects all over London, still with a small team of volunteers and a couple of musicians." They considered the possibility of working with younger people and children and started the Youth Group in 2003.

In 2006, Magpie was successful in achieving a grant of £500,000 over five years from the Big Lottery Fund's Reaching Communities programme (in the lottery's first year of operation). Like the very first grant in 1994, this grant was a big step change once again for the organisation and enabled the trustees to appoint a full-time General Manager in 2007. Avril became a full-time employee and the company found a new home with an office at the Churchill Theatre, Bromley in 2008. It was the first time in its 22-year history, the organisation had two full-time employees, and it was fitting Magpie had an office base in the theatre where it held its first public theatre performance in 1994.

Wider recognition for Magpie and Avril

Over the past 30 years, Magpie has won numerous awards and several articles have been published about it. Many students have researched Magpie as a case study for their degree courses. It currently hosts 10-15 students on work placements every year.

Magpie won the Bromley Business Award in 2015 in four separate categories, beating hundreds of other companies with far greater financial turnover.

Avril has given talks and workshops at venues including the Royal Society of Medicine, Royal Academy of Dance, Sadler's Wells, Rotary clubs, Third Sector and Social Impact conferences in London, Suffolk, Yorkshire, Leicester, Birmingham, Sweden and Bangladesh.

Opening doors for those who dare to dream

Avril now has a team of 20 talented, dedicated and driven individuals she has built up over the years. Magpie delivers 350 sessions every year working with a range of partners and organisations.

Under Avril's leadership, the organisation has touched the lives of thousands of young and older people with learning disabilities and their support networks, giving them an opportunity to tap into their creativity and allowing them free expression.

It has not been easy. "I have to drive forward to make things happen and keep going because I believe in it." But Avril knows it has been worth all the effort when she sees "how people can flourish and what they can do to become independent". Magpie is all about "opening doors for people," she adds.

Avril truly believes that being disabled should not stop someone from becoming a professional dancer. In 2011, Magpie commissioned Counterculture Partners to undertake a viability study into setting up a new performance company for dancers with learning difficulties. The study found that there was a distinct lack of progression and training pathways for these dancers.

In 2014, Magpie Dance's Highfliers became the first company of its kind. Dancers have to audition to have a chance to get selected. The programme has been modelled so as to capture the excitement and vigour of a dance training company. The year-long training company is fully funded so that dancers can attend free of charge, accessing funding worth £8,500 per person for the year. It opens up a pathway for these dancers to train, with the aim that they will get paid to perform on mainstream stages in future.

Avril tells me about a 15-year-old girl who progressed well through the organisation, did a peer-mentoring programme and underwent in-house training on Magpie's Inclusive Dance Practice Training programme, where she learnt alongside other trainees how to facilitate inclusive dance sessions. Avril remembers with pride how "she did better than some of her fellow trainees without learning disabilities" and is now a "fantastic volunteer" who also enjoys paid work at Magpie when the right opportunity presents itself. This young lady is now also a Highflier as part of a unique initiative that provides further opportunity for her talent to flourish so that she can take her skills to the next level.

Lessons learnt and advice

- "You need to have drive, resilience and really believe in what you do."

"The key to success is to surround yourself with experts who know what they are doing. Doing it all yourself is not a sustainable strategy."

CHAPTER 32

Pooja Kapur
– Founder, Towards A
Special Cause – India

Pooja has personal experience of the debilitating impact of living with a disability. TASC is a unique initiative that helps children and adults in deeply disadvantaged communities to be rehabilitated, educated and vocationally trained, so they can become more productive members of society.

Pooja spent her early years in Bangalore, Delhi and Chennai. After completing her post graduation in advertising and marketing, she spent two years working for *The Times of India*, a daily broadsheet newspaper firm. She got married and was working with the advertising agency J Walter Thomson when she became pregnant with her first child. She took a three-year break from work before briefly joining a recruitment firm in Dubai, where she was then living.

Mumbai calling

At around the time of Pooja's second pregnancy, her husband was given an exciting opportunity by his employer which involved returning to India and living in Mumbai. She recalls the day she landed in Mumbai heavily pregnant with her second child and her daughter who was three years old.

As their taxi drove them from the airport to their destination, they travelled through an area that to this day is home to street dwellers, with a busy road on one side and the train tracks on the other. "I was very taken aback by the number of children who were living on the streets. It was a stark contrast to what life had been like in Dubai, or anywhere else I had lived."

That was the catalyst that made Pooja see that she was ready to do something different. She started writing for social causes. She contacted the editor at *Femina*, an Indian magazine publication, to ask if she could write on a freelance basis for them. "I knew they wouldn't be interested if I wrote on a social issue, so I made my first article deliberately provocative: about the topic of married women who are attracted to men other than their husbands. That certainly got the editor's attention!" She became a freelance writer for a few other publications, including her previous employer, The 'Times of India, for a period of five years while her children were still very young.

Not long after moving to Mumbai, Pooja started an initiative called Towards a Special Cause (TASC). Her motto is: *Every cause is special. Impact any cause close to your heart, wherever, whenever and in whatever way possible.* For 15 years, TASC has been driven by the two-member team of Pooja and her identical twin sister Payal, who first joined to support Pooja's quest but gradually "became the brains behind an effort that was led solely by my heart." But first of all, here's a glimpse into how the seeds of TASC were sown many years earlier in Pooja's and Payal's childhood.

Living with disability

Pooja had a first cousin who was severely disabled. Despite having a loving family around her, the environment was "pretty hopeless, with people relying on prayers" back then due to the lack of any proper developmental opportunity for the child in a small town. Growing up in such close proximity to someone whose condition deteriorated with each passing year left a lasting impression on Pooja. She witnessed the devastating impact it had on her aunt who, until her daughter's death in her teens, was unable to leave her side for long.

Deeply affected by the plight of her cousin's condition, Pooja wanted to find a way to help others like her. She came across what used to be called the Spastic Society of Tamil Nadu, now renamed as Vidyasagar. She volunteered as a teacher but "did not last very long".

"I found that I could not really contribute as positively as the (specially trained) teachers there. It was a humbling experience as I discovered I was not equipped to make an impact in that way." Pooja decided, instead, to focus on helping people in organisations like that one to do their jobs well.

Becoming an enabler for those doing good

"TASC does not aim to focus on any one cause, but to reach out to multiple causes in our own little way, " says Pooja. When she finds a cause that resonates with her, she personally supports it and "shouts about it" to others, including corporates, who may be able to help by donating funds or providing expertise or help in some other way. TASC does not directly handle money and has no intention of becoming a charity or NGO.

Initially, some people were sceptical of Pooja's TASC initiative. Her deliberately scattered approach was out of the norm. However, over time she has gained enormous personal credibility having had a positive impact on hundred of lives. Some of the many causes she has supported are connected to helping people who are blind, deaf, deaf and blind, as well as vulnerable children and adults. TASC has provided invaluable support to orphanages, old age homes, shelters for street children and vocational centres for women. She has also helped rehabilitate women and children afflicted with HIV, cancer sufferers and acid attack victims. Above all, she is passionate about helping those she supports to find employment and become independent members of society.

Educating donors and making charity more sustainable

Pooja explains that the problem some organisations face is that their funding support tends to be ad hoc and volatile. These organisations need to build a corpus, but donors don't always appreciate the importance of the financial self-sufficiency that it can provide. She talks about the need to educate donors. "People don't understand that even NGOs have costs that need to be covered. It doesn't help that some NGOs have given the sector a bad name."

A unique personal crusade

Would turning TASC into an NGO give it greater legitimacy and reach? "Being an NGO would allow TASC to have a clear record of the significant amount money we have helped to channel towards the causes we have supported over the years," Pooja says. On the other hand, she enjoys tremendous credibility because TASC is almost entirely her personal crusade to make the world a better place for a growing band of deeply disadvantaged people in India. People who support her know that she has no axe to grind and no "personal association" to any of the causes she supports. This she believes is rare in India and what makes TASC different.

How does Pooja promote her chosen causes and connect them to people who might be willing to help? "Until six years ago, pre-social media, I was doing things on a very small scale, and mainly on a personal level (in terms of financial and other help). Spreading awareness was not as easy as it is today. (Corporate Social Responsibility) CSR policies were also a bit different in those days. Now (thanks to social media) there is a bigger support group and the working style has also evolved. I prefer to work with organisations that are not too well known."

One of her favourite organisations is Mann, which runs a school for children with severe challenges. What drew her to it was the fact that its founder was a teacher that Pooja had met and impressed her. Children at the school with learning difficulties caused by conditions such as autism, Down's Syndrome and Attention Deficit Hyperactivity Disorder (ADHD) were all from neighbouring slums. These children from poor families had been "disregarded, often tied up" for their own safety whilst the parents went about their daily grind.

Those running the school realised there was no way these children could independently travel to and from school and so invested in a school bus. But they had underestimated the cost of running it for 40 children and so had to seek funding.

Pooja remembers approaching an established entity that was created to help the likes of Mann to scale up, but they disappointingly turned down the funding request for short sighted and bureaucratic reasons. Organisations like Mann can only continue to do vital good work, helping individuals that are so often ignored by society, thanks to personal donations and initiatives like TASC.

Mann is now five years old and has two schools. The standard of care and education is so high that there is demand from parents who are willing to pay for their child to be enrolled. "But to their credit, they have stayed true to their original cause and continue to focus on kids who cannot afford to go to school, but need help the most."

What criteria does TASC use to decide which causes it will continue to support? "I prefer to support an organisation that wants to grow or improve in some way," says Pooja. "I choose not to continue with organisations that show no growth, or are receiving generous funding, but use it only to sustain what they already have."

Has Pooja ever been tempted to grow TASC's reach by getting others to join her? She admits that there have been people who wanted to help on an ongoing basis, but she declined their offer because she recognises that she does not have "a very structured way of operating" and tends to have a "varied workflow". This, she thinks, can be hard for a third person to understand, although she welcomes ad hoc support and people getting in touch to help out as and when they can.

Payal has been part of TASC for almost 12 years. While Pooja handles most of the work centred out of Mumbai, she lends support to the work in Mumbai and also runs her own initiatives for TASC in Gurgaon, Delhi and Bangalore. They have an excellent understanding and working relationship that would be hard to replicate with someone else.

Lessons learnt and advice

- "Whenever I have a bad day, I think about all the people that Payal and I have interacted with – hoping and intending to help – and remember how blessed most of us are compared to them. I am humbled by how they live life to the fullest and smile despite their lot, grateful for whatever little they get."

- "A downside of doing what we do is the realisation that I can never ever be 100 per cent happy because I have been sensitised to too much suffering. I don't think I can live a single day without being subconsciously aware of it."

- "Doing whatever little I can helps a little, but I am also aware that what I do pales in comparison to what actual caregivers and people who live and die for a cause do. No matter how much we do, there is always more that needs doing."

"Encouraging vocational training has always been a large part of TASC's objective. No education is complete unless it gives individuals the tools to earn a living from it. Enabling employability for those whom we support is key."

CHAPTER 33

Shoma Bakre
– Founder, Let's Do Some Good – India

Putting her life as a successful entrepreneur behind her, Shoma is now putting her wealth of experience in the corporate world to good use by creating an independent platform that enables greater collaboration towards a common cause.

Shoma comes from a "very humble background" in Assam. Quite early on in her life, she made the decision that she would put something back into the community. Before she got married she was a teacher in Assam and then moved to the US after marrying her husband, whom she considers as one of her early mentors.

Once in the US, she did an MBA and then got a job at Applied Materials, a global leader in the semiconductor industry. Shoma credits her husband with how she came to be the highly organised person she is now. "I was overwhelmed by the amount of work I had to do," she recalls. "He told me to observe the personal assistants of the senior executives to see how they get things done." It was a hugely important early lesson in organising busy schedules and breaking things down into more manageable goals to achieve a larger objective.

The journey from entrepreneurship to doing some good

Shoma returned to India for a short stint along with her husband and their very young children, but she knew within a year that she did not want to live anywhere else. Shoma went on to successfully start up the business information service provider, EmPower Research (covered earlier in this book) with three others and then sold it for a good price seven years later.

"When EmPower was sold, the biggest plan (for me) was to give myself a break and then work in social service", remembers Shoma. Since her return to India, she had been financially contributing to causes close to her heart. She had the option to continue in a leadership position at the enlarged business that now included EmPower, but chose not to. The idea of doing nothing, however, gave her "sleepless nights".

Instead of enjoying a quiet retired life, she launched herself into a number of ventures, including setting up a creative cooking website and publishing a cookbook. She also went on to make a documentary on successful alternative models of education for underprivileged children, a longstanding dream of hers. For this, she featured three non-profit organisations that catered to underprivileged sections of society. While making the film, Shoma enjoyed valuable interactions with men, women and children from slum communities, as well as NGO staff who worked with them, which gave her a flavour of "the grassroots level".

During this shoot for the documentary, Shoma interacted closely with Mom Bannerjee, the founder of Samridhdhi Trust, a non-profit organisation that aims to give underprivileged children a chance to access mainstream education. Shoma realised during the making of the documentary, there were many different entities with essentially the same objectives that were doing the same things but not collaborating. "They were reinventing the wheel on a daily basis, when actually working together made sense and would have saved time and resources, enabling them to tackle what is an enormous problem so much better", says Shoma.

Her meeting with Mom proved fortuitous as both were on the same wavelength. Shoma explained her vision of becoming a facilitator for different organisations to work together towards a shared purpose. She and Mom decided to create a symposium and invite the who's who of CSR and non-profit work in Bangalore to brainstorm ideas for encouraging greater collaboration in the not-for-profit sector.

Shoma was able to get a corporate sponsor for the all-day event, which was attended by representatives of over 100 organisations. As these organisations saw themselves as being in competition with each other, they were unlikely to collaborate unless there was a neutral platform that enabled them to co-operate.

Becoming the facilitator for greater collaboration

The symposium happened in December 2013, and within weeks they had created the Bangalore Effective Education Task Force (BEETF). The aim was to bring together different entities working in the field of education of children of the urban poor. Today, BEETF has over 65 partner organisations comprising of corporates, NGOs, Non Profit Organisations (NPOs), academia, and many individuals working in this sphere.

Shoma was instrumental in making this happen and she was encouraged to put her name behind an initiative that would bring people who want to do good together. This led to the formal creation of Let's Do Some Good Foundation (LDSG) in March 2014. Shoma believes that through LDSG she is doing what she always wanted to do, but on a larger scale.

What was it like to suddenly operate in a world so different to the corporate sector she had been more accustomed to? Shoma considers her mentor to be Mr Warrier, CEO of Manipal Foundation, an organisation that provides funding support for social initiatives, such as healthcare, education, vocational skills and women's empowerment. He was instrumental in influencing her to form LDSG as a Trust. He also helped her to see that in the not-for-profit world of social change, you are targeting very different things. "There is no exit plan, it is very long term, the outcomes are sometimes less tangible and fulfilment is very different."

Punching above her weight

From humble but ambitious beginnings, LDSG now leads the strategy and planning for BEETF. It partners with multiple stakeholders who are together tackling huge socio-economic challenges that stem from extreme poverty in urban places like Bangalore. By working in collaboration, it is helping to join the dots between children's education, women's empowerment and the upliftment of entire communities. It is also helping those coming out of education to find jobs.

Now Shoma mentors young people who are interested in doing some good, but not just as a hobby. She only has time for those who are in it for the long term.

Shoma gives me an example of her informal mentoring. A student of architecture tried to contact her several times, but she did not take her seriously at first. The young lady persevered, however, until she was finally able to speak to Shoma. She had started an initiative to teach young schoolgirls from underprivileged communities about hygiene issues and had come up with a design to build low-cost toilets.

LDSG already had its own Build a Toilet programme, and was in the process of a toilet renovation project at a school. Shoma connected the young woman to the right people on the team and left it to her to prove that she was serious. "She took my guidance very well and successfully executed two large toilet projects in government schools for LDSG. She has gone on to become the Miss India 2016 First Runner-up and also won the "Beauty with a Purpose Award" at the pageant for the work she has done with LDSG. She continues to demonstrate the same zeal for the cause that she showed me. She really took the lessons to heart and I consider my time spent on mentoring her well spent."

Over a year ago, Shoma was invited more formally to mentor female entrepreneurs by an organisation that is a global network of women entrepreneurs. She also mentors female professionals.

I ask Shoma what gender differences she thinks exist in the workplace, when it comes to attitude and professionalism. "At EmPower, when we started the company, 70-80 per cent of the employees were women," she explains. "So there was a gender imbalance of having too many women and over the years we had to consciously hire males in order to bring a better gender balance."

Amongst the female employees, she found "the utmost professionalism: they'd give 150 per cent because: a) they were eager to prove that they were no less than a man; b) they wanted to do their work and then play the other roles they had to play; and c) they were very loyal".

Shoma goes on to add, "We also provided an environment that was conducive to them working flexibly. We didn't micromanage them, we gave them the freedom to do their jobs."

On the flipside, Shoma observed that women generally were less likely to claim credit for their work. "Women are in a rush to deliver on targets, so they can go on to doing their other work. But they are not very comfortable talking about their own achievements."

Are women more sensitive to criticism? "Women are constantly struggling to get to their position, so any criticism hurts more. Perhaps men don't face the same issues." She hastens to add that these are personality traits, rather than an indication of professionalism in the workplace.

Finding the right balance

"Working for yourself, whether in the corporate sector or in the non profit sector, requires discipline. Just because no one is breathing down your neck does not mean there isn't self-imposed pressure."

Shoma has a group of volunteers who work with her. When there are so many causes to support and so many people wanting her advice, she is aware of the danger of spreading herself too thin. So she remains goal oriented, focused on her chosen cause, highly organised and methodical. She is closely involved in all aspects of the running of LDSG and personally funds the running costs of the organisation.

What about work-life balance? "I have an amazing husband, teenage children who are quite independent and reliable hired home help", all of which allows Shoma to do what she does. She loves to travel and it is when she is away that she takes a self-imposed break from all work-related issues.

Lessons learnt and advice

- "Identify what is dear to your heart and how you want to make a difference."
- "Identify what your constraints are that are stopping you from doing what you want to do. Is it time, money, health or something else?"
- "Look for opportunities or go to a network of friends and family."
- "Give yourself a small thing to do. You don't need to start with a bang or with a grand plan that overwhelms you."
- "Once you've started something don't give up. What you give is nothing compared to what you will get back."
- "Find fun, innovative, interesting ways to raise money to help your chosen cause."

"What I really want to do is to create an environment where everybody feels like doing some good, so that everybody can find the one cause they want to support and choose to make a difference."

Ganga's story as told by Vaidy Singararaman – Co-Founder, The Ganga Trust – India

Ganga was a woman ahead of her times. Her strength of character, generosity of spirit and relentless positivity, even in the face of the most trying circumstances were the gifts she gave to all whose lives she touched. Vaidy is continuing his mother's legacy through his work with The Ganga Trust and The Spinal Foundation, India, which are helping to rebuild broken lives.

Ganga was born in 1925 in a small village about 300 kilometres from Chennai. A naturally bright girl, she walked a long distance each day to get to school. Ganga went to a girls' school until the eighth grade, after which the only available school was for both boys and girls. Coming from a very conservative, traditional Tamilian family, her parents decided against sending her to that school, which prematurely ended her formal education.

Whilst still in her teens, Ganga found herself married to Singararaman from Chennai. They went on to have six children: two boys and four girls. Vaidy was the youngest and born 23 years after the eldest son. According to Vaidy, "Her thirst for learning never left her, as she continued to read magazines and newspapers both in Tamil and English. Her lack of formal education never stopped her from holding an intelligent conversation on almost any subject."

Vaidy's upbringing was humble: the family of eight slept in a single room. He recalls his mother's overwhelming sense of pride when her older son was offered a job at a bank at a salary far exceeding her husband's. This was especially welcome news as their life savings had been spent on Vaidy's older sister's wedding. He remembers Ganga's utter devotion to her family. "Despite the constant battle with not having enough money, the quality of care and food never faltered. She always found a way to make it interesting for the family."

Ganga was an extrovert. "She was a people person and extremely generous to a cause that touched her heart. Giving came very naturally to her." Vaidy remembers her giving money away to anyone who was in need with a sad story, even if it was all that she had.

Ganga was also a strong woman with a very clear philosophy on life, which she instilled in her children. *Aaghavendiatha Paaru* is Tamil for 'look ahead and focus on what needs to be done now, rather than living in the past'.

In 1975, Vaidy was only ten when his brother became seriously ill and later his father passed away. "Finding solutions was her forte," he says of his mother. On another occasion, they were struck by multiple deaths within the extended family, days before the wedding of one of his sisters. Hindu tradition dictates that in the event of a death in the family, any happy occasion must be postponed for at least a year. Ganga, despite her strong faith and religious beliefs, took a pragmatic view and decided to press on with the wedding. Her view was that there was little to be gained by putting off an event that they had invested so much time and resource into.

In many ways, Ganga was a woman ahead of her times. "She lived her life as a proper Hindu but didn't care too much about what others thought, so long as it was something she believed in." Living the life of a widow can't have been easy at a time when women had no financial self-sufficiency, and especially once her children had grown up and left home. "She liked her independence. She loved being alone. She loved beaches and nature with all its flora and fauna," says Vaidy of his mother. He believes he has inherited many of her traits: traits that served him well in his own life.

The night that changed lives

Vaidy was a student at the Indian Institute of Management, Bangalore (IIM-B) and in his second year of the two-year postgraduate programme. He had been out celebrating with his classmates after a couple of them had received good news about scholarships.

It was well after 2am on the morning of 28th of July, 1990. Vaidy and two of his friends were on the first-floor balcony just outside the dormitory rooms. He was perched on the balcony wall, something he had never done before. At one point he reached down to pick up his footwear, but lost his balance and plunged to the ground beneath, falling through the big gap in the wall that exists even today.

It all happened in the blink of an eye, but Vaidy remembers it like it was yesterday and in slow motion. One of his friends, also sitting on the wall, stretched out his hand to try and break Vaidy's fall. "Mercifully, I did not take his hand, as he would have come down with me. My back landed on the mini-iron railing that held the edges of the flooring together. It was this that did the damage, even though I was fully conscious and there was not even a scratch anywhere on my body. At that time, I had no idea of the importance of the spinal cord. I had read about it briefly years ago in school. As soon as I landed on the ground, I realised that my legs were not moving, nor was my core. Below the upper part of the chest, my body appeared to have become paralysed."

Vaidy's companions came racing to his aid. He was carried to the back seat of a car and rushed to hospital. His friends had minimised his injuries through a combination of luck and presence of mind. The way they had carried Vaidy and transported him in the car had avoided putting any further pressure on his spine. "Greater awareness and proper handling of the injured person at the scene of an accident is instrumental in saving lives and reducing loss of mobility," says Vaidy.

That night changed Vaidy's life forever. The initial diagnosis was that he would be in a wheelchair for the rest of his life, confirmed by a specialist two days later. "When the specialist mentioned these effects, I just asked to be left alone for five minutes. I did not cry or sulk or think along the lines of 'why me?' or 'why this type of a challenge?'"

"I did not look at the past. I just crossed out a few aspects that may no longer be possible, including sex in its fullest sense, and made a decision to do everything that I could to help the process of recovery. One other decision that I made very early on was that I was going back to IIM-B to complete the course."

"On July 30, early evening when my Amma (mother) walked into the room, I told her that it was best to look ahead and I would like her also to do so immediately. I also asked her to show her usual courage in facing up to reality. What I remember is she did not cry at all, and she immediately assessed the situation and agreed with me."

The long road to recovery and rehabilitation

What followed was six long months of physical recovery and rehabilitation. Bangalore did not have the requisite facilities and so the decision was made to move Vaidy to Christian Medical College (CMC) in Vellore, more than 200 kilometres away. "As the ambulance was about to move out, I cried, not for the injury and its aftermath, but for the fact that I would miss the fun and frolics with my classmates."

"In CMC, Vellore, my next stroke of good luck came in the form of Dr Suranjan Bhattacharji, who epitomises everything that is and can be good about life. Suranjan is one of the earliest to specialise in the field of Physical Medicine & Rehabilitation in India (PMR). In 1990, he was considered among the top five in the world in the field of spinal-cord injury treatment and rehabilitation. He had offers from hospitals around the world and at a price of his choosing. He opted to stay in Vellore and has now devoted four decades and counting in working for the physically challenged in India."

Vaidy was indeed fortunate to be in the care of an excellent team of doctors, nurses and physiotherapists. His body had to relearn the many things that he had previously taken for granted: simple things like sitting up, brushing his teeth and eating independently. Having his hair washed was a treat.

"In any rehabilitation post a spinal cord injury, almost nothing is routine and nothing can be taken for granted; however, simple the task. Hard work will help you to learn each task and improve your efficiency over time. Every task in day-to-day to life had to be re-learnt, as well as newer needs for mobility, bladder and bowel management and skin care."

Vaidy drew confidence from his mother's "courage and smiles". He also speaks reverently of Dr Bhattacharji and his "messianic calmness" and the healing effect he had on him.

Vaidy was in good hands during his stay at CMC Vellore, having spent six months in their care, but the real challenge would be remaining independent once back in the real world. Vaidy's first goal was to head back to IIM-B to complete his MBA along with his classmates. He missed his friends and was painfully aware that they would all be graduating in the summer of 1991. He wanted more than anything else to spend the last three months of the academic year on campus with them.

At first, the management of IIM-B was unsure they were equipped to let Vaidy back on campus. There had been no precedent of taking on a student with a physical disability. But Vaidy was not a new student; he simply wanted to finish what he had started.

In December 1990, Dr Bhattacharji wrote to the institute outlining Vaidy's condition, his needs and why he believed Vaidy was ready to return. Vaidy found a copy of this letter amongst his late mother's meagre possessions 21 years later. "You read the letter and you realise how visionary and thoughtful Suranjan was, and still is."

A new adventure for Ganga and Vaidy

Dr Bhattacharji's intervention was clearly instrumental in facilitating Vaidy's return to IIM-B. But his hope of doing three terms worth of coursework in one was too optimistic. He would go on to stay at the institute for an extra year graduating a year later than he had originally planned.

Vaidy firmly believes his mother never doubted his ability to cope independently back on campus. Nevertheless she asked permission to accompany him and stay with him for her own peace of mind. Ganga was given her own room in the dormitories alongside Vaidy's on the ground floor. Their rooms overlooked the 'quadrangle'; a hub of activity, where the parties and other student gatherings happened.

How did Ganga find life on campus surrounded by students? "She loved it and thrived being around young people. She had always enjoyed reading and there was no shortage of books or magazines on campus. She took long walks and made friends with the teaching faculty and other members of staff."

It was a proud moment for Ganga when her son graduated in 1992. And at the age of 66, she got to live like a student in one of the most prestigious academic institutions in the country. It was a dream-come-true for someone whose love of learning and reading surpassed her own formal education that ended at the age of 13.

Back in the real world

Earning a highly regarded qualification, it turns out, is not enough to get a job. Vaidy discovered that most employers were not willing to risk taking on a candidate in a wheelchair. Vaidy was vehement that he only wanted a job on his merits, not because someone felt sorry for him. He tells me of the time he had started a working at a respected financial institution. On his third day, he was handed some paperwork that would have effectively classified him as handicapped and so eligible for inclusion in their disabled employees' quota. He resigned.

It was not an easy time and money was short. His mother remained a pillar of support, believing with the utmost conviction that things would work themselves out. Vaidy got a job as Head of Business Research at *The Hindu*, an Indian broadsheet newspaper, where he remained for 12 and a half years. He later went on to work as Risk Manager at Sundaram Asset Management, a respected manager of mutual funds in India, where he remained in full-time employment until March 2010.

Giving back

In 2009, Vaidy got talking with Elango, one of his dearest friends from the IIM days, and another friend Girish, from his time with *The Hindu*. They discussed the plight of people with disabilities in India and their lack of inclusion into society and so decided to set up The Ganga Trust. In doing so, Elango and Vaidy were translating into action what Dr Bhattacharji had told them in 1990: "As alumni of IIM-B you will be in a position of influence in due course. You must do your bit to enhance the quality of life of persons with disability."

The original objective of the Trust was to bring together top quality individuals who would pledge their support and provide the money needed to meet some key objectives. It involved working with other organisations dealing with patients with spinal cord injury around the country.

In 2010, Vaidy moved to working on his day job on a part-time basis so that he could spend more time on The Ganga Trust. In March 2013, he gave up paid employment altogether to focus all his attention on it. He now also works for The Spinal

Foundation, a pan-Indian self-help group for people with spinal cord injuries. He makes regular visits to other patients with spinal injuries at the Rehab Centre in CMC Vellore to advise and inspire them.

One of their core aims is to set up ground-level infrastructure, especially for people in remote parts of India. The data collection mechanism is poor, but Vaidy estimates that there are 10-15,000 new cases of spinal cord injuries each year. The vast majority will not get the care they need. The correct treatment, starting from the time of the injury and long after rehab is completed, can ensure that the patient lives a reasonably normal life. Greater awareness amongst ordinary people plays a huge role in ensuring there is greater inclusion of people with physical disability into society.

Vaidy believes firmly that education plays a big part in how people respond to people in wheelchairs. IIM-B had initially been very reluctant to let Vaidy back in because he was in a wheelchair. But the students took things in their stride, partly because they had known Vaidy before his accident, and more so because of his positive attitude towards life. Once you get past seeing the wheelchair, it is still the same person you once knew.

Today Vaidy works tirelessly for his cause. He has participated in multiple fundraising wheelchair marathons and networks, relentlessly aiming to reach more of those whose lives have been blighted by spinal cord injury. He does not take a penny as salary and is currently living off his modest savings built up during his working life. His work for The Ganga Trust and The Spinal Foundation is a labour of love; a promise fulfilled to his mother, Ganga, who had wanted him to simply put something back into a world that had been kind to him.

Ganga passed away in 2002 after a brief illness. Before she died, she helped Vaidy secure further independence by helping him to buy a small piece of land where his purpose-built house now stands. He credits his mother for his unshakeable faith in the future, refusal to dwell on the past and complete unwillingness to indulge in any form of self-pity.

Lessons learnt and advice

Ganga's life's lesson has been passed on to Vaidy: "Look ahead and focus on what needs to be done now, rather than living in the past."

CHAPTER 35

An untold story

There is one leading lady whose story I am unable to publish because of reasons personal to her. I have known her for around five years. She is someone who lights up the room with her presence, quick wit and sheer *joie de vivre*. You can imagine everyone turning to her in a crisis because she would know what to do and do it calmly without any drama. She is deeply compassionate with a big heart and an infinite capacity for love. I am proud to have her as a friend.

She spent over three decades in a job that she "loved every minute of, even if it was hard work" and had wanted to do since the age of six. She told me about the personal sacrifices she made so that she could prove she was "just as good as any of the men" who often, especially in the early days, resented her presence. She retired when she knew that she had "ticked all the boxes at least once" and was ready to do something different. Aside from being there for her elderly mother, whose health is waning, she now works part time in yet another job that most of us would shy away from.

The death of three of the closest members of her family some years ago left a wound that would not heal. Organising their funerals was such a traumatic experience, she promised herself that some day she would work in that field and do it in a more empathetic and compassionate way. That is one of the many things she now does post-retirement, and is by all accounts busier than ever, still making a difference to people's lives as much as she did when she was working.

Lessons learnt and advice

- "Try to be nice to each other and don't see other women as competition (especially when you work in a male-dominated industry)."
- "Keep your perspective; don't sweat the small stuff. We are all so tiny in the scheme of things that most of the daily traumas are not worth considering."
- "Take time each day to enjoy the positive things in life, instead of always worrying about the things you have to do."

"My only regret is that I cared more about how I was perceived at work about being a single mum. I wish I had spent more time just being a mum."

Life lessons: finding your place in the puzzle

For every story that becomes public, there will be thousands that remain untold. Every one of us has a story to tell. Like things of great beauty in Nature that are quite unaware of their own loveliness, some of the most interesting stories belong to those who may not consider themselves worthy. How well do you know the people in your life? How well do they know you? How well do you know yourself?

Beginnings, journeys and finding adjacent pieces that fit

We need others on our life's journey. Without them, we will be no more than a solitary piece of the jigsaw puzzle. Every one of the stories in this book highlight the importance of at least one other person, without whose support or guidance the individuals featured would not be where they are today. Whether they be parents who instilled the right values and stood by their offspring, a supportive husband, a business partner, a sibling, a close friend or a mentor.

The most beautiful of partnerships, be it in life or in a business, occur between people with complementary skills, a mutual respect and a shared objective. When you find someone like that in your life, celebrate, for you have found a piece of the jigsaw puzzle that fits neatly with you, completing at least a small part of your picture.

The ecosystem that we are born into — our family, the neighbourhood we grow up in, the schools we go to — has a major influence on the person we become. Those who are not fortunate enough to be born into a safe and loving family will, not surprisingly, find it much harder to find their way in life.

Although beginnings matter, the journey is more important. However difficult and out of our control our beginnings might have been, there is one thing we can control: the choices we make at every turn. Along the way, we will come across a multitude of people and circumstances. It could take just one of those to change the entire trajectory of our life, but only if we are alert to it and make the right decision at that particular point in time.

Knowing when to act, when to wait and when to move on

If you have a dream, an idea or a passion, the worst thing you can do is to do nothing. Imagine never finding out what might have happened had you taken the first step to bringing it to life. Success often comes from trial and error. Start small, plan ahead and aim big. Goal setting and periodically tracking your progress against targets helps to ensure that you are not going off track.

Having taken that first tentative step and several more after, how long should you wait before giving up or changing tack? What if you gave up just when things were, unbeknownst to you, about to turn around? If this is your livelihood, how long can you keep going if you are not earning enough? Remember, you need to combine passion and purpose with pragmatism.

How do you know how much of your progress (or lack of it) is due to what you are doing and how much is down to other things outside your control? What are you actively doing to make things happen, even while you are patiently waiting for that breakthrough? You know that it can take time to make a success of a new venture, so give yourself a time frame before you review things again. Stay informed, keep learning and evolving, and go with your instinct.

You may have reached a juncture in your life where you are no longer thriving. The passion has ebbed away and you are not learning anything new anymore. You are going through the motions and the things you once loved, no longer fill you with joy. This may be a clear sign that you are ready for a change.

You may have been in the same career for years, or only ever fulfilled the role of a housewife and mother. It can be scary to go from the relative safety and familiarity of the old to the risky unknowable nature of the new. Which is why a catalyst is often needed to push us out of our comfort zone. What is your catalyst? Or can you simply catalyse yourself to make that change?

Dealing with calamitous change

Sometimes life deals us a hand that changes everything. It could be a personal event, like the death of loved one, a divorce, an accident that puts you in a wheelchair for life, or a natural disaster that destroys everything you have built. Resilient people don't dwell on things that cannot be changed. They look ahead and make a judgment on how they can best fit into the altered reality of their life. They consciously focus on positive things and that they can still control. They are also willing to start again, learn anew and embrace change.

Deanne and Masao rebuilt their Hooplovers business from scratch in Australia after the Japanese tsunami destroyed their livelihood. Raga had to change her business model when she discovered it was not resilient enough. A number of the ladies faced financial hardship and single parenthood after a divorce. They each found a way to reinvent themselves and are now much happier and financially more secure. Anna was dealt a double blow when she discovered both her boys were autistic, but instead of buckling under the pressure, she has gone on to do the best for them and thousands of others. Vaidy's life changed overnight 26 years ago when he fell from a balcony. Now he is racing on wheels to help others in India whose lives have been broken due to a spinal cord injury.

What next?

So change has been thrust upon you or you've decided you need a change, even if you have no idea in what direction it will take you.

Keeping your senses alive and mind open will help you make the right decision. No one else can answer some of life's difficult questions for you because they have not been part of your personal journey, and they may not be travelling with you when you face the consequences of your decision.

Sometimes life moves at such a pace that there is no time to stop and reflect before choosing which way to turn. Think of people who have to make life-changing decisions every single day of their life. They have to make up their minds in a split second with imperfect information and very little idea of how exactly things will turn out. These are times when, at a deep subconscious level, we must draw on the things we have learnt in the past, make a judgment of what might happen in the future and then go with our instinct.

You may not always make the right decision. Even flawed decisions teach us things about ourselves and about others. Once you are prepared to learn from your good and bad decisions, you will come to understand that they have all had a part to play in getting you to the place where you belong.

Seek advice, get help, and network

Both in life and in business, knowing what you are good at and also recognising that you cannot be good at everything will save you a lot of time, heartache and expense. It will help you to focus on the things that you do best, and where you have both potential and the ability to improve.

Successful people know their own strengths and are not afraid of admitting their weaknesses. They will most likely compensate for these weaknesses by having someone on their team who fulfils that role much better. Complementary skills are developed in teams by first admitting you need someone who can do the things you can't, and then by being prepared to allow them to do their job well.

Finding the relevant peer group in the community you live / work in will go a long way to alleviating the loneliness that sometimes comes from working for yourself. These are groups of people quite separate from your friends and family. Such networks, communities or tribes, as my ladies refer to them, are places where you can bounce ideas off each other and share experiences with like-minded people. Learning from others' experiences can help you to leapfrog mistakes you might have committed.

There have been a few mentions of people who want something for nothing. People who may take advantage of your relationship with them or exploit your inexperience at negotiation. People who want to "pick your brains" but have no intention of doing business with you. Try not to be one of those people. It is unfair on those who are trying to make a living but are too polite to say no to free riders. Instead, learn to both give before you ask for something and to collaborate. Collaboration is the not so secret win-win transaction where no money changes hands, but you still create a formula for mutual success.

Money and Profit are not dirty words

You may not mind helping people for no personal reward because you are a naturally giving person who is not in it for the money. But people don't generally value things they get for free. There is a greater commitment to making something work or see a problem through if there is a personal investment, however small.

Potential customers and rivals may also measure the worth of the service you are offering by how much you charge. Price discovery and the self-knowledge of the value of the product or service you are selling are both important aspects of running a successful business.

If you fail to charge your customers the correct price, you may not be able to cover all your costs. You may run out of cash and be unable to pay for the costs the next time. Soon you will either be in in debt (which you may find hard to pay down) or out of business – neither is an appealing option.

Whatever your line of work, if you are good at it then you owe it to yourself and your clients to make enough money so that you can afford to stay in business. Kaye learnt to say no to people who were taking up her time so she could devote it to clients who actually needed and valued her services.

You may want to look beyond simply surviving. If you want your business to thrive, you need to be prepared to invest in it to make it flourish, giving your clients an even better experience. This may involve making personal financial sacrifices for the greater good of the business.

A focus on making a profit should not stop you from offering potential customers "free" tasters or rewarding loyal customers with the occasional 'freebie'. This is particularly true when you are tapping into a new market or offering a service that people don't yet know they need or how to value.

In Amrita's and Bindu's case, they went a step further. They built tremendous goodwill and became considered as thought leaders by inviting young mothers to free seminars on mother and baby issues, even though it had no direct link to their core business.

Claire, Deanne, Jo and Kiran had to offer their services for free before they could prove to potential clients of the benefits to them. Swapna offers free samples of her cakes so people know what they are buying before they buy. Sangita and her co-founders priced their services really low as a way to get US clients interested. They knew that once they had seen the benefits, they would be back for more and willing to pay up.

Dealing with rejection and failure

There is only one way to prepare for rejection in later life; it is to start as early as possible. Try new things, meet people outside of your close network of friends and family, volunteer, travel, do apprenticeships, read, listen to people who have done amazing things in their own lives and battled adversity. The more you are willing to put yourself out there and take a risk, the more you will get a taste for it.

There are few simple ways of pre-empting, responding to and dealing with rejection.

- **Ask nicely**. It may surprise you to learn that most people find it hard to reject someone who is polite, charming and genuine.
- **Accept their negative decision with grace**. This is not the same as giving up. Anger, resentment or petulance in the face of rejection does not win friends or customers.
- **Ask for feedback**. If someone says 'no', it helps to understand the reasons why. And it may even give you an idea as to what you could do differently next time, giving you a better chance of a 'yes'.

- **Rejection is personal**, no matter what anyone says and however impersonally the news is delivered to you. But it does not mean that you are unworthy. It simply means that it was not the right role, the right time or the right person for you. Accept it and move on. The quicker you do this, the sooner you will find the right one for you.
- **Find a reason to keep going**. When life has kicked you when you are down one too many times, it takes courage to get up and try again. Having someone in your life that depends on you often means you have to keep going. You don't know how strong you are until you have no choice other than to be strong.
- **Find your personal champion**. Most people who become successful despite repeated setbacks attribute it to one or more people in their lives who believed in them completely, even when no one else did.
- **Take time to stop and reflect**. Out of rejection and failure, sometimes comes blinding realisation. Perhaps you have been going down the wrong road all along and your destiny lies elsewhere. When you find it, you will be thankful for all those 'no's' that once made you feel like a failure.

Rejection is a part of life, no matter how successful we become or how old we are. How we handle it, both as a giver and a recipient, will define us as individuals. If you have never been rejected, chances are you played it too safe.

Finding Success

Your definition of success is personal to you, and it may or may not have anything to do with money. You may have noticed none of the women in my book used money as a barometer of their progress, or even their eventual success once they had "arrived".

There is an easy to remember acronym of the four key ingredients for success:

- **T**alent
- **H**ard Work
- **A**ttitude
- **T**ime

Money, like success, will be a by-product of all the hard work, smart thinking and passion you put into your business (or life). How you conduct yourself will have a lasting impression on the legacy you create and leave behind, even after you are no longer involved in the business.

The entrepreneurs in our book ran their businesses like they would their household budget – with care and always ensuring the people who worked for them were paid on time. The owners of the business did not really get paid salaries until the business was on a much firmer footing and even then, it was probably not commensurate with what they might have earned in corporate jobs. In fact, they strongly advise you not to start a business if your motivation is simply to have an easy life and earn as much, or more than, you would in a corporate job.

There are many sacrifices you may have to make if you want to create something from nothing. It is no different to having a baby who will demand more of you than you ever thought you had in you. So long as you give it your all, bring others in to help (remember the African proverb: it takes a village to raise a child) and nurture your business like you would your child, it will pay you dividends and outlive your own personal legacy some day.

Mental toughness

Our ladies variously advise us to be authentic, confident, passionate, strong, realistic and humble. Possessing talent or academic achievements cannot guarantee success. In fact, nothing can. There are many others out there looking for the same things that you are and with whom you might have to compete. Some of them won't want to see you succeed.

Competition is a good thing. It proves that the thing you are going after is worth fighting for. It should make you raise your game. Always treat your competitors with respect, even if they may not do the same for you. Badmouthing a competitor is never a good trait; it shows weakness. Let your own strength shine through, instead.

When you succeed, not everyone will like you. Some will want to bring you down. Social media makes it easier for people to throw negativity at others from behind the curtain of anonymity. It takes humility and a certain steeliness of resolve to deal with criticism, constructive or not. Mental toughness must be cultivated with just as much fervour as all the other skills that go with becoming successful.

Valuing those who help complete your puzzle

From the second we are born into this world, our lives will be touched by words and actions of others. Those who cared for us and nourished our minds and hearts; the friendships we formed in our formative years; the teachers who inspired us to learn, or those who bored us senseless putting us off education; even the people who were unkind to us leaving us with a life-long memory of how small they made us feel.

Sometimes people will come into our lives for a reason that may only become apparent to us much later. They may leave a powerful impression on us and move on, leaving us bereft. Sometimes a strong friendship may peter out with time as we grow apart and develop into two people who are no longer on the same wavelength. We will have our crushes, even fall in love. Some day we may decide to settle down with someone we hope we will share the rest of our life with. Every one of those interactions will change us and move us along on our lifelong journey.

However successful you become, making time for family and friends, showing them how much you value their support is the emotional nourishment they need to keep them going. The same goes for loyal and hard-working members of your team at work. A business has several stakeholders: employees are amongst those who are often overlooked.

Business owners who treat employees as just numbers and a cost, viewing them as dispensable and easily replaceable, are unlikely to enjoy long-term success. Some make the mistake of thinking that throwing more money at someone who is threatening to leave will make them stay. When you do that, the message you are sending is that you reward employees who are disloyal and are seeking to go elsewhere.

We have read the experiences of the ladies who went on to set up successful businesses employing hundreds of people. Personality fit and the right attitude was more important than qualifications or previous experience when they recruited. Once they were hired, these employees were given specific training that was designed to make them do their job in a way that matched the culture and vision of the organisation. They won the loyalty of their workforce because they empowered them and made them feel valued. Make sure you work for someone who does the same for you. Or if you happen to be the boss, remember your people are your greatest assets. They are the ones who will help you complete the picture in the puzzle of your life that relates to the success of your business.

There are too many individuals who are excluded from productive society for one reason or another, be it because they are physically disabled or have learning difficulties, or because they happen to have spent most of their adult life as a wife or mother with no other work experience. It is not that difficult to find a way to harness the productive capacity of such people who really want to work. Once there is a collective will within an organisation to embrace people of different abilities, it is possible to have a workforce that is diverse, empowered and immensely loyal. To make this a reality, the vision needs to come from the top, and it needs the buy-in of all those below. Perhaps you could be one of those change makers.

Be multi-dimensional

One of the enduring lessons learnt by some of the ladies in this book was not to burn out, and to find time for yourself so you remain energised and enthusiastic. When you are totally focused on a job, being busy all the time becomes a barometer of success. But if you wear yourself out, you are not doing yourself or your customers any favours. They say change is often as good as a rest. Finding time away from your work so that you can unwind, recharge your batteries and emerge refreshed is essential.

Everyday life is a house with many rooms in it: a room for the family; another one for work; a third one for friends; and so on. There are some who don't believe in these distinctions, claiming that they in effect have an open plan house where family, friends and work intermingle. But for most people, life is better managed in compartments. Developing other dimensions to your personality and exploring new compartments in your life is a conscious act of evolution.

Exploring interests, finding hobbies, meeting new people, travelling to places off the beaten track, occasionally doing things that scare us or we don't like, these are all things that open our minds and make us more tolerant, empathetic and compassionate.

They also make us braver and more interesting. But most of all, they help to prepare us for the next wave of change that will inevitably sweep into our lives. A change that may well irreversibly alter the picture that we have worked so hard, piece by piece, to build over time.

The tapestry of our life may yet have many more pictures for us to complete. Let us rejoice in every opportunity and be prepared to once again embark on a new journey to find where we belong.

ACKNOWLEDGEMENTS

There are many people I want to thank for the roles they have played in helping this book take shape. The idea of writing a book came to me when I was inspired by the writings of my friend and start-up guru Sanjay Anandaram. His initial guidance and encouragement proved invaluable in setting me on the right track. Thanks also to Sudeshna Shome Ghosh for your input on how best to structure my book to make it relevant to today's reader.

I am grateful to Nainesh Jaisingh for getting me my very first interview with Namit Malhotra, Founder and CEO of Prime Focus, one of the world's most respected global media services companies. Although his story could not be published, it gave me a glimpse into what is possible and I am deeply grateful for the time he spent with me patiently answering my questions.

I owe huge thanks to Jackie Barrie for publicising my project to her network of successful women who are running their own businesses, a number of who are in my book. Many thanks also to Mridula Kaul for putting me in touch with so many interesting and inspiring women.

Thank you to Anil Thomas, Mala Thapar, Nigel Pitchford and Nilima Bhat for introducing me to amazing women who I hope will also become my lifelong friends. Thank you to my publishers Leila Dewji and Ali Dewji at I_AM Self-Publishing who have impressed me greatly with their professionalism from day one.

Last but not least, thank you to everyone who is featured or mentioned in my book. Aside from providing me with the best quality raw material I could have wished for, their stories have inspired me to boldly set forth on my own brand new journey to discover where I now belong.

ABOUT THE AUTHOR

Rohini is preparing to become a business and life coach. She has two decades of experience working within a global equity team as analyst and fund manager, investing on behalf of charities, institutions and wealthy individuals. She commits up to ten hours per week teaching hoop-dance fitness to all age groups with a view to donating her earnings from that to good causes. She is also the founder of Raindrop Campaign, a UK charity focused on the education of underprivileged children in India. She lives in London with her husband and children. This is her first book. She has been blogging for about a year under the name Ro's Random Musings.

Lightning Source UK Ltd.
Milton Keynes UK
UKOW02f2040181116
287990UK00002B/2/P